5294

POET IN

Federico García Lorca was born into an educated family of small landowners in Fuente-Vaqueros in 1898. A poet, dramatist, musician and artist, he attended the university at Granada, where he acquired a fine knowledge of literature. In 1918 he went to the Residencia de Estudiantes in Madrid and during his long stay there he met all the principal writers, critics and scholars who visited the place, which was then a flourishing centre of cultural liberalism. In 1928 his *Gipsy-Ballad Book* (*Romancero gitano*) received much public acclaim. In 1929 he went to New York with Fernando de los Rios and his volume of poems, *Poet in New York* (*Poeta en Nueva York*), was published posthumously in 1940.

On his return to republican Spain he devoted himself chiefly to the theatre as co-director of La Barraca, a government-sponsored student theatrical company that toured the country. He now wrote few poems, but those few include his masterpiece *Lament for Sánchez Mejías* (*Llanto por Ignacio Sánchez Mejías*; 1935), a lament for a dead bull fighter. He wrote some classical plays, pantomimic interludes, puppet plays, including *La zapatera prodigiosa* (1930), and three folk tragedies – *Blood Wedding* (*Bodas de sangre*; 1933), *Yerma* (1934) and *The House of Bernarda Alba* (*La casa de Bernarda Alba*; 1936), published by Penguin in one volume under the title *The Rural Trilogy*.

In 1936, just after the outbreak of the Spanish Civil War, he was murdered at Granada, in mysterious circumstances, by Nationalist partisans.

Describing Lorca's art, the eminent critic Raymond Williams wrote: 'In his discovery of forms, he is strikingly original, and yet he seems to range, with creative confidence, over the many possibilities of the modern dramatic tradition. It is an intensely personal and identifiably national achievement, yet it makes us look again, with new eyes, at the forms now available to us . . . In the intense power of his creative effort, against the negatives of the wasteland, he extended dramatic possibility, beyond the conventional frontiers.'

POET IN NEW YORK

FEDERICO GARCÍA LORCA

TRANSLATED BY GREG SIMON
AND STEVEN F. WHITE
EDITED AND WITH AN INTRODUCTION
BY CHRISTOPHER MAURER

PENGUIN BOOKS

PENGUIN BOOKS

Published by the Penguin Group
Penguin Books Ltd, 27 Wrights Lane, London W8 5TZ, England
Viking Penguin, a division of Penguin Books USA Inc.
375 Hudson Street, New York, New York 10014, USA
Penguin Books Australia Ltd, Ringwood, Victoria, Australia
Penguin Books Canada Ltd, 2801 John Street, Markham, Ontario, Canada L3R 1B4
Penguin Books (NZ) Ltd, 182–190 Wairau Road, Auckland 10, New Zealand

Penguin Books Ltd, Registered Offices: Harmondsworth, Middlesex, England

First published in Spain, under the title *Poeta in Nueva York*, 1940
This English translation first published in the USA by Farrar, Straus, Giroux, New York 1988
Published simultaneously in Canada by Collins Publishers, Toronto
First published in Great Britain, by arrangement with Farrar, Straus and Giroux Inc.,
19 Union Square West, New York, NY 10003, USA, by Viking 1989
Published in Penguin Books 1990
10 9 8 7 6 5 4 3 2

Printed in England by Clays Ltd, St Ives plc

Frontispiece: Federico García Lorca at Columbia University, October 1929

The translators of Poeta en Nueva York
owe a very great debt of gratitude to
Andrew A. Anderson, Thomas Colchie,
Daniel Eisenberg, Christopher Maurer,
Mark Strand, and John Witte.
G. S. / S. F. W.

The editor is grateful for the kind
assistance of Andrew A. Anderson,
Philip Cummings, Daniel Eisenberg,
Manuel Fernández-Montesinos,
Mario Hernández, María Estrella Iglesias,
John K. Walsh, and the Committee on
Latin American and Iberian Studies,
Harvard University.
C. M.

Acknowledgments are due to the
following magazines in which several
and more recent versions of these
translations appeared for the first time:
Northwest Review, Paris Review,
Porch, *and* Third Rail

Contents

Introduction

García Lorca would remember his stay in New York (June 1929–March 1930) as "one of the most useful experiences" of his life, and in fact the nine months that he spent in New York, Vermont, and Havana changed his vision of himself and of his art.

This was his first visit to a foreign country, his first encounter with the racial and religious diversity of a democratic society (Spain had been governed for almost six years by the dictator Primo de Rivera), and his first, frightening glimpse of urban crowds. The importance of all this for a poet who had always been deeply interested in social problems can hardly be underestimated.

New York also served him as a great school of the theater. His own career as a playwright was just beginning: only two of his works had been staged in Spain, and a third, *The Love of Don Perlimplín*, was in rehearsal when it was closed down by government censors. The trip to New York gave him the opportunity to distance himself psychologically from the Spanish theater of his day and to judge it as a whole. Two important experimental works, *Once Five Years Pass* and *The Audience*, were begun in the New World. "One must think of the theater of the future," he writes to his family. "Everything that now exists in Spain is dead. Either the theater changes radically, or it dies away forever. There is no other solution." He must have been greatly interested in the way the theater was organized in New York. He had had no previous contact with a commercially viable tradition of university or repertory theater, and it is likely that American groups like the Neighborhood Playhouse, the Theatre Guild, and the Civic Repertory Theatre served as models, after his return to Spain, for the drama groups he himself founded during the first years of the Spanish Republic. He was fascinated by the black revue, as much perhaps by the black audience as by the performers, and he must have remembered all this after his return to Spain as he sought to save the Spanish stage from the expectations of middle-class audiences. What plays he saw in English no one knows. The language barrier would not have prevented him from absorbing what seemed interesting or novel about the nonverbal aspects of drama.

Few critics have written about Lorca's life in New York without insisting that he felt depressed and isolated. The Spanish poet Rafael Alberti tells us that *Poet in New York* was written by "a lonely poet . . . lost amid docks and avenues and skyscrapers, returning in nostalgia and anguish to his little room at Columbia University." This is surely the impression given by the poems, but the letters which Lorca wrote to his family show that he was surrounded and affectionately cared for by Spanish-speaking friends, old and new, who were either living in the city or passing through. Because his command of English never advanced as far as syntax and grammar—he was a simple collector of "English" words, from *spaghettis* to *shishpil* (sex appeal)—his only American friends were those who already knew something of Spain and of Hispanic culture: the editor Herschel Brickell, the journalist and translator Mildred Adams, and an imaginative young writer from Vermont whom Lorca had met in Spain, Philip Cummings.

The trip to New York and Cuba took place at an extremely difficult moment in Lorca's life. Toward the end of July 1928, the thirty-year-old poet confessed to a friend that he was going through "one of the worst crises" he had ever known:

I now realize what it is that the erotic poets mean by the fire of love, and I have come to this realization precisely when I need to cut it from my life in order not to go under. It is stronger than I suspected. If I had continued to nourish it, it would have done away with my heart. You [say that you] had never seen me so bitter, and it is true. I am full of despair and feel listless and crippled. This has made me feel extraordinarily humble. We'll see if I can accomplish what I want to with my poetry, and if I can finally cut these terrible bonds and return to the happiness I once felt.[1]

He is alluding to the end of his affair—one of the most important of his life—with a Spanish sculptor, eight years younger, Emilio Aladrén. The poet's love had not been reciprocated: Aladrén seems to have played cruelly with Lorca's emotions and used him to further his own career. The affair was a subject of gossip in Madrid, and Lorca's disorganized, impulsive way of life was now a source of worry to his parents, who hoped that in New York he would learn to administer his time, and their money, more wisely. The poet would study English at Columbia University and prepare a book about his American experience.

The "emotional crisis" to which Lorca refers in several letters of 1928 had been strangely aggravated by the critical success of his third book of poems, *The Gypsy Ballads*. The *Ballads* had drawn national attention to his poetry for the first time, and had made him known as a "gypsy poet," a term which had once amused him but which he now found revolting. The contrast between his public "image" and his private self, both as a writer and as a man (for Spanish society could not accept his homosexuality and several of his closest friends chose to know nothing about it), was becoming ever more grotesque and painful. The beginnings of fame made it all but unbearable. As early as January 1927, over a year before the *Ballads* were published, Lorca told a friend how irritated he was by "the myth of my gypsiness":

People confuse my life and character. And this is the last thing I want. The gypsies are nothing but a theme. I could just as well be the poet

---

[1] Letter to José Antonio Rubio Sacristán, quoted in *Federico García Lorca escribe a su familia desde Nueva York y La Habana (1929–1930)*, ed. C. Maurer, in *Poesía* (Madrid) 23–24 (1986), p. 11.

of sewing needles or hydraulic landscapes. Furthermore, this "gypsy" business gives me an uneducated, uncultured tone and makes me into a "savage poet," which you know I am not. I just don't want them to pigeonhole me. I feel they are trying to chain me down.

Salvador Dalí, who had been Lorca's close friend since 1925, but from whom Lorca had now become estranged, sensed the anguish the poet was feeling. Soon after the *Ballads* appeared in print, he wrote to reassure him:

I love you for what the book reveals you to be, which is just the opposite of the reality that has been invented by rotten people everywhere: the dark-haired gypsy lad with the heart of a child, etc.: that whole decorative, unreal, nonexistent Lorca . . . who could only have been dreamed up by "artistic" swine who know nothing of the little fish and the little bears and the soft, hard, and liquid contours that surround us.[2]

But Dalí's opinion of the *Ballads* themselves only deepened Lorca's depression. In the same letter he reproaches Lorca for having written a book that is "bound, hands and feet, to the old poetry," one which "cannot move us and cannot satisfy the desires of modern readers." The indictment goes cruelly on for several pages. The *Ballads* are filled with clichés and stereotypes, "all the usual ideas about things." The book's imagery only serves to reinforce a "traditional" view of reality, in which things are compared with one another or evoked sentimentally, but never allowed to be *themselves*. The minute hands of a watch, Dalí explains,

only begin to acquire real value when they stop pointing to the hour and, losing their circular rhythm and the function assigned to them arbitrarily by our intelligence . . . escape from the watch and become

[2] Ian Gibson, *Federico García Lorca 1. De Fuente Vaqueros a Nueva York* (Barcelona: Grijalbo, 1985), p. 568.

a new bodily joint, in the place that corresponds to the sex organs of bread crumbs.

Another old friend, Luis Buñuel, had complained, rather less eloquently, of the *Ballads'* traditionalism:

The book has a certain dramatism for those who like that sort of flamenco dramatism. It captures the spirit of the classic ballad, for those who want the classic ballad to survive from one century to the next. There are even some magnificent, extremely original images, but there aren't very many, and they are all mixed up in a plot which I find unbearable, one which has filled the beds of Spain with menstrual blood.[3]

Buñuel was writing to Dalí, whom he had long hoped to separate from Lorca. That winter the painter invited Buñuel to Figueras, where they wrote the script of *Un chien andalou*, filmed in Paris in the spring of 1929. Although he may not have seen it until much later, Lorca knew of the film, and believed that Dalí and Buñuel were conspiring against him. In New York he is said to have told Ángel del Río: "Buñuel has made a little shit of a film called *An Andalusian Dog*, and the 'Andalusian dog' is me."[4]

All this forms part of the troubling biographical background of *Poet in New York* and helps to explain Lorca's abrupt departure from the poetic manner of his earlier works. For many reasons, *Poet in New York* marks a turning point in his poetry. It is his first book inspired by the city, rather than the country, and the only one not tied in some way to Andalusia. The New York poems are also the first that directly address social injustice. The book is as innovative formally as it is thematically: although there are several poems in hendecasyllables, and parts of the "Ode to Walt Whitman" are written in fourteen-syllable alexandrines, free verse is used more extensively here than previ-

[3] Luis Buñuel, *Obra literaria*, ed. Agustín Sánchez Vidal (Zaragoza: Ediciones de Heraldo de Aragón, 1982), p. 30.
[4] Ibid., p. 33.

ously. The major stylistic change, however, lies in the nature of Lorca's poetic imagery.

By October 1928, Lorca was aware of having entered a new stage in his development as a poet. Dalí's observations on the *Ballads* seem to have provided the stimulus for a lecture entitled "Imagination, Inspiration, Evasion,"[5] in which Lorca discusses two types of poetry, the first of which he had now transcended. There is, he writes, a poetry that is content to discover unsuspected relations between objects and ideas: this is the poetry of "imagination," whose eternal symbol is the great baroque poet Luis de Góngora. The "imaginative" poet is bound by the laws of "human logic, which is controlled by, and cannot break free of, reason." It is imagination, Lorca explains, that has "discovered the four points of the compass and the intermediate causes of things." The poet uses it to explore and describe the universe, and to "construct a tower against mystery and against the elements." But there is a second type of poetry, the poetry of "inspiration," which permits poet and reader to *acknowledge* mystery and to "evade" reality. In "inspired" poetry, the traditional metaphor yields to the *hecho poético*, the "poetic fact," an image which seems as inexplicable as a miracle, for it is devoid of any analogical meaning. Based on the *hecho poético*, and bound together by *la lógica poética*, the poem becomes a "self-sufficient entity without reference to any reality outside itself."[6] This is one of Lorca's aesthetic ideals in *Poet in New York*, a work which has often been described as surrealistic.

Lorca had known of surrealism at least since 1925, and, like all the major Spanish poets of his generation, was familiar with André Breton's first manifesto, but it should be noted that in

[5] F. García Lorca, *Conferencias*, ed. C. Maurer (Madrid: Alianza Editorial, 1984), Vol. II, pp. 10–31.

[6] Derek Harris, *García Lorca: Poeta en Nueva York* (London: Grant and Cutler, 1978), p. 12. This is the best guide to Lorca's book available in English. It includes a useful bibliography.

his lecture of 1928 (repeated several times in New York and Cuba) he explicitly rejects the use of dreams and of the subconscious as a technique for "poetic evasion." Such an evasion "may be very pure, but it is not very clear. We Latins want sharp profiles and visible mystery. Form and sensuality." In *Poet in New York*, Lorca would avoid the automatism which Breton had advocated in 1924. The critic Derek Harris has written that Lorca "exploits the surrealist freedom from moral, aesthetic or rational constraint, but only as a means of production for his imagery. He does not seek to establish the condition of surreality where conscious and subconscious experience combine."[7] The "surreality" of *Poet in New York* is not an end in itself, nor does it have much to do with the epistemological impulse that lies behind the work Dalí was doing in 1927–28: Lorca could not have shared Dalí's longing to discover "reality" by liberating things from their usual "functional" meaning and emotional charge.

In *Poet in New York*, as, to a lesser degree, in the *Ballads*, traditional metaphors appear, in a disconcerting way, among hermetic images. The windows of Wall Street, for example, are compared to a *columbario* (literally, a dovecote or a cemetery niche). The grilles on automobiles make it possible to say that they are *cubiertos de dientes* ("covered with teeth"). Roses bound together for shipment to the city are "manacled" flowers, and the rage of the blacks is "fire [that] slept in the flints." A "harp of living tree trunks" lines the shore of Havana, where the poet hears the "rhythm of dried seeds" (sound of the maracas). These metaphors are not very different from those which occur in the *Ballads* and in earlier works. But a far greater number of images can be elucidated only after patient study of their semantic connotations throughout the *entire cycle* of New York poems. Much of the imagery has no rational "explanation" whatsoever, and some critics have responded, perhaps a bit vengefully, by dis-

[7] Ibid., p. 14.

mantling the poems one by one, charting Lorca's "poetic universe," and taking inventory of the animals, minerals, and plants which appear most frequently in these pages. There have also been attempts to show that certain images are "positive" and others "negative." These critical approaches, which often pay lip service to the multivalency of Lorca's images, have led to wildly divergent readings of certain poems. "Abandoned Church" has been said to deal with the lost promise of the blacks of Harlem; with "the drama of Christian hypocrisy"; with sexual frustration; and with the loss of religious faith. No "true" reading is possible, and reference to other poems does not lead us any closer to a "correct" interpretation. This is surely an example of the sort of poetic "evasion" mentioned earlier.

Poet in New York is both a condemnation of modern urban civilization—the spiritual emptiness epitomized by New York—and a dark cry of metaphysical loneliness. García Lorca once considered entitling the book *Introduction to Death*, and the "death" alluded to is both spiritual and physical, both that of the poet and that of the world around him.

The central and most dramatic death is that of the poet himself; not the author of the book, but the first-person "subject" of the poems: a protean, self-conscious figure who has been aptly described as "Prometheus, prophet and priest." The difference between this figure and García Lorca himself, between the "empirical author" and his poetic persona, should not be overlooked. The family letters will remind the reader that not all of *Poet in New York* is best read as a lyrical autobiography. The boyish, carefree writer of the family letters and the tragic and sometimes Whitmanesque "self" or "subject" of the book of poems are two masks, or two voices, of one of the most complex spirits of modern European poetry.

García Lorca died without seeing the book published, but in the 1930s he presented many of the unpublished poems in the form of a lecture to audiences in Spain, Argentina, and Uruguay. In this lecture, which has influenced all recent critical readings of the book, Lorca does his best to identify himself with the "I" of the poems. Minimizing the distance between life and art, he creates a partly fictitious narrative of how he wrote the poems, and interprets his own book, rather too narrowly, as an attack on the United States, a country bereft of spiritual greatness. The title *Poet in New York* was meant to sound paradoxical: how *could* a poet survive there? Lorca's statements to the Spanish-language press in the years following his return from the United States share the anti-American tone of the lecture (an anti-Americanism that had become quite common in the Spain of the early 1930s):

New York is something awful, something monstrous. I like to walk the streets, lost, but I recognize that New York is the world's great lie. New York is Senegal with machines.

The only things that the United States has given to the world are skyscrapers, jazz, and cocktails. That is all. And in Cuba, in our America, they make much better cocktails.

Besides black art, there is only automation and mechanization.[8]

It would be wrong to doubt the sincerity of these remarks, but the scope of *Poet in New York* is certainly wider than Lorca led his first listeners to believe. The "poet" does indeed condemn white urban American civilization, but that civilization is merely the most immediate, clearest possible image of the spiritual poverty of twentieth-century man. The "sleepless city" of the poems is late-night Manhattan, all its lights ablaze, but it is also the vigil of modern man in quest of the cosmic *meaning* of so much suffering. The wrathful poet-priest presides over the destruction

[8] From interviews in 1931, 1933, and 1936, reprinted in García Lorca, *Obras completas*, Vol. III (Madrid: Aguilar, 1986, 22nd edition), pp. 502, 513, 675. This book is referred to in the notes that follow as *OC*.

of city streets: "Cobras shall hiss on the top floors. / Nettles shall shake courtyards and terraces" and social injustice will meet its just reward. But he does more. He looks beyond circumstance to the edge of the unknown, in order to understand the pain around him; and much of that suffering does not seem to have any "social" or "moral" explanation.

Everyone understands the pain that accompanies death,
but genuine pain doesn't live in the spirit,
nor in the air, nor in our lives,
nor on these terraces of billowing smoke.
The genuine pain that keeps everything awake
is a tiny, infinite burn
on the innocent eyes of other systems.

In Lorca's poetic awareness of these "other systems"—birds and insects, idiot children, tree trunks, water and sand, the moon and planets—lies a measure of the greatness of *Poet in New York* and of all his poetry. No Spanish poet ever made his readers more conscious of the sinister, alien qualities of things. In the same poem ("Blind Panorama of New York") he remarks:

We forget that the mind has boroughs
where Chinese and caterpillars devour the philosopher.

Several years later, in a new lecture on artistic inspiration, he would return to the same thought: artistic inspiration is more precious than intelligence. The latter "is often the enemy of poetry, because it limits too much, and it elevates the poet to a sharp-edged throne, making him forget that ants could eat him or that a great arsenic lobster could fall on his head" ("Play and Theory of the *Duende*"). The sharp edges, the *aristas*, of that throne, the throne of rational thought, are analogous to those of Manhattan. If there *is* a moral explanation for the suffering Lorca sees in New York, it lies in this: man's ignorance of, or indifference to, "the other." The redemptive role of the poet is to remind the reader in memorable speech of the limits of human thought: to remind him of the "living earth" under the "patterns" and pavements of the metropolis and of the "otherness" that lies *beyond* human speech. The stubborn hermeticism of much of *Poet in New York* may be seen as a refusal to ignore that "otherness," whose most visible symbol, in all Lorca's work, is the earth—dumb, terrifying image of two inseparable mysteries: life and death.

A recent critical account of *Poet in New York* identifies its three major themes as "social injustice, dark love, and lost faith."[9] Their common element is the alienation, or "otherness," just mentioned. The "social" aspect of the book is easiest to grasp; *Poet in New York* condemns capitalist society and all that it seems to entail: an anthropocentric world view; the degradation of nature; indifference to suffering; the materialistic corruption of love and religion; and the alienation of social groups, particularly the blacks.

The poems about the blacks were the first that Lorca wrote in the New World. Little more than a month after his arrival in New York, Lorca went to explore Harlem with the black novelist Nella Larsen, and dreamed of writing a book which would "sound an entirely new note" about the black experience. He had arrived in New York in the last days of what is now known as the "Harlem Renaissance."[10] "Standards and Paradise of the Blacks" is an attempt to define the blacks through their aesthetic and vital norms, above all through their longing for the "deserted blue": the blue of infinity and the blue of ancestral African skies, "blue of a night without fear of day," night of the blues, coal-black blues of the blackest members of the race. The object of their longing, the "paradise" named in the title, is a sort of

---

[9] Richard L. Predmore, *Lorca's New York Poetry: Social Injustice, Dark Love, Lost Faith* (Durham: Duke University Press, 1980).

[10] On Lorca's view of black culture, see C. Maurer, ed., *Federico García Lorca escribe a su familia desde Nueva York y La Habana (1929–1930)*, pp. 143–50.

celestial graveyard, where torsos lie dreaming, returning to the void.

The vision entitled "The King of Harlem" is both protest and warning: protest (as Lorca states in his lecture) that "the blacks do not want to be black"; warning that the blood raging under their skin ". . . will flow / on rooftops everywhere, / and burn the blond women's chlorophyll, / and groan at the foot of the beds near the washstands' insomnia, / and burst into an aurora of tobacco and low yellow" as the black race overwhelms the white. What Lorca saw of racial discrimination in New York troubled him for the rest of his life. In 1933 he told an interviewer in Buenos Aires that he wanted to write a tragedy about the blacks, but could not do so until he had fully understood "a world shameless and cruel enough to divide people by color when in fact color is the sign of God's artistic genius."

The blacks' loss of cultural identity—their supposed nostalgia for their ancestral roots—is analogous to the poet's own. *Poet in New York* owes some of its uniqueness to the way that the "social" domain reflects the private, and poems of protest mingle with elegy. The poem entitled "1910 (Intermezzo)" is an elegy for the poet's own lost childhood, a time when he was less preoccupied with suffering, sexual problems, and death, and was able to stare wonderingly at the simple, immediate realities of rural life: the horror of "the bull's muzzle, the poisonous mushroom," a religious engraving of St. Rose of Lima, the family garden, "where cats devour frogs," the "pony's neck," and "an incomprehensible moon." By now, he has lost his sense of self. Only once, far from the city, in rural surroundings that evoke the world of his childhood, does he speak of having regained his "old voice":

Ay, *my love's ancient voice,*
ay, *voice of my truth,*

ay, voice of my open side,
when all the roses spilled from my tongue . . .

That voice has now turned to "tin and talc" ("Double Poem of Lake Eden," written, perhaps, near the Vermont talc mine he visited with Cummings. Embedded in almost all the poems are faintly identifiable fragments of American reality).

Other retrospective poems—"Your Childhood in Menton," "Fable of Three Friends to Be Sung in Rounds"—seem to have grown from the emotional crisis and the feelings of abandonment and betrayal which preceded the trip to New York. Critics have tried in vain to identify the person to whom "Your Childhood . . ." is addressed. Some argue that the poet is addressing himself. But the bitterness of lines 9–12 seem directed to a lover who has spurned the poet's norms of homosexual ("Apollonian") love:

What I gave you, Apollonian man, was the standard of love,
fits of tears with an estranged nightingale.
But ruin fed upon you, you whittled yourself to nothing
for the sake of fleeting, aimless dreams.

The "Fable of Three Friends . . ." is too full of private allusions to hold much meaning for the reader. It is a response to the affair with Aladrén, and a poetic "settling of accounts" with two others who somehow took part in it. Here, as on eight other occasions in the book, the poet speaks of his assassination ("I knew they had murdered me").[11] The many images of mutilation and murder point to the loss of "identity" alluded to earlier.

• • •

[11] "The effect of this . . . is to lend a weird pathos to the squalid occasion in 1936 when Lorca was taken out to a road near his native Granada, and literally assassinated . . . [But] Lorca's poems were not his epitaphs. They were poems, and the result of reading them into Lorca's death is to prettify a very unpretty business and to make the poems look rather slight into the bargain." Michael Wood, "The Lorca Murder Case," *The New York Review of Books*, Nov. 24, 1977, p. 38.

Poet in New York is divided into ten chapters, the headings of which provide a narrative framework and allow the book to be read as the story of a psychological voyage. By section IV the poet has moved from the city to the rural scenario of Vermont. But he is as haunted by death in the "rural" poems of sections IV, V, and VI as he is in the "urban" ones. The transmutations we read of in "Death"—the longing of the horse to be a dog and of the swallow to be a bee—reflect the desire for otherness that governs all creation; a desire defeated, as it always is in Lorca, by death. The poet himself, who would be a "burning angel," must pass, like the rest of creation, through the "plaster arch,"[12] the narrows of death, and the void. Life is seen in this book as metamorphosis: Ovid read in a deathly light. *Son mentira las formas* ("Shapes [or forms] are a lie"), the poet exclaims in another poem. In life and in death, everything flows. Behind the broken windowpanes of an abandoned country house, about to be overpowered by grass and weeds, the poet senses "sand struggling with water" ("Ruin").

Soon it was clear that the moon
was a horse's skull,
and the air, a dark apple.

The "timeless doors" of the earth lead back to the "blush of the fruit," and even the dead have no rest: thus the conversation between two dead men in a Vermont graveyard, who sit up to hear the howling of a dog: "Cancer's three nymphs" have been dancing, and someone else is about to join them. Even here there is an echo of childhood. One of the dead men says he has "loved a child / who had a tiny feather on his tongue, / and we lived inside a knife for a hundred years." In his lecture "On Lullabies" (1928), Lorca speaks of a cradle song from southern Spain:

[12] Harris (p. 41) suggests that the poet is thinking of "the plastered-up niche of a Spanish cemetery."

Lullaby, little boy,
in the country we'll build
a tiny hut
and live inside.

"Danger is near," Lorca says, explaining the lullaby. "We must make ourselves smaller, tiny . . . Outside, they are waiting to hurt us. We must live in a tiny place. If we can, we will live in an orange, you and me. Even better, in a grape!" In the desolation of New York, the orange (or grape) becomes a knife. No religious consolation is offered, here or anywhere else in the book; man is as alienated from God as he is from his childhood, or from the rest of creation. "The world [is] alone in the lonely sky" ("Christmas on the Hudson").

Lorca's vision of the impermanence or emptiness of forms—forms abandoned in the senseless flux of life: the "husks of insects," lost gloves, or cast-off suits of clothes—gives rise to one of the most frequent and most untranslatable images in the book: the *hueco*: void or hollow, space or emptied space. The atmosphere of New York is riddled with *huecos*: "There are spaces that ache in the uninhabited air." In *Poet in New York*, as in all of Lorca's writing, abstract concepts and perceptions turn into astonishingly *tangible* poetic figures. Master of the elegy, able to compare what *is* and what is *not*, the object and its "void," Lorca gives color and weight to the notion of annihilation itself, an example of the "sharp profiles and visible mystery" noted in the lecture on imagination mentioned earlier.

In the void that is at the center of his swirling images, in the eye of the storm, in the resonant hollow of the well, is an absent child. No psychological explanation can account for the verbal adventure of *Poet in New York*, but figures like "Little Stanton," the "Little Girl Drowned in the Well," and the dead son in "Abandoned Church" testify to the poet's sexual frustration and his inability to engender a child. It is as though the pent-up aching water of the well—water which "never reaches the sea" or, more literally, has no outlet or never disgorges—were unspent life. The child who cannot leave the well is present in one of Lorca's earliest books of poetry, *Suites* (1920–23):

Song of the Unborn Child

You have left me on a flower
of the water's dark sobs!
The weeping I learned
will grow old,
trailing its bustle
of sighs and tears.
Without arms, how can I push open
the door of the Light?
Some other child has used them
to row his little boat . . .[13]

The anguish of *Suites*, which was not published during Lorca's lifetime, suffuses much of the New York poetry. Lorca quotes from the book in *Once Five Years Pass*, a play whose homosexual protagonist dreams of the son he will never engender.[14] For both the "Young Man" of the play and the subject of *Poet in New York*, the unengendered child becomes the child *within*, the child borne into adulthood; and, in a way typical of surrealist art, the child within is also an image of the poetic imagination and of the poetic voice which the writer has lost and cannot recover.

The theme of homosexuality is now acknowledged to be of fundamental importance in *Poet in New York*, and the "Ode to Walt Whitman," which was first published in a limited, private

[13] *Suites*, ed. André Belamich (Barcelona: Ariel, 1983), pp. 201–3.
[14] For an excellent discussion of the "unengendered child" in this play and in the rest of Lorca's work, see José Ángel Valente, "Pez luna," *Trece de Nieve* (Madrid) 1–2 (1976), pp. 191–201.

edition, is Lorca's most extensive, and most ambitious, treatment of that subject. Here the thought of death lends urgency to love and seems to grant man the freedom to love as he chooses:

Tomorrow, loves will become stones, and Time
a breeze that drowses in the branches.

And thus man can guide his desire "through a vein of coral" or through a "heavenly naked body." One of the unresolved tensions in the book, as in Lorca's life, is this: on the one hand, grief for the "unengendered child"; on the other, the calm certainty, expressed in the "Ode," that not all men were destined for procreation:

. . . it's all right if a man doesn't look for his delight
in tomorrow morning's jungle of blood.
The sky has shores where life is avoided
and there are bodies that shouldn't repeat themselves in the dawn.

Despite the clarity of lines like these, the "Ode" is a strangely ambiguous poem. A rather confusing distinction is drawn between the "classical" homosexual (the Whitmanesque "camerado"), and those whom the poet would exclude from the symposium: "urban faggots," "slaves of women," pederasts: "all the greedy and neurotic riff-raff who form [part] of what is often called the 'gay scene.' "[15] The latter group has no right to invoke Whitman as its patron. The "classical" element is rather more difficult to characterize. Social concerns blend here with sexual ones in a way that is characteristic of Lorca: American capitalism has somehow corrupted Whitman's vision of love. Paul Binding has explained the analogy implicit in the "Ode": "the failure of homosexual life to live up to the Whitmanesque image of it is inextricable from the failure of American society

[15] Paul Binding, *Lorca: The Gay Imagination* (London: GMP, 1985), p. 139.

to live up to Whitman's social pastorals for it."[16] Like *The Audience*, Lorca's drama about homoerotic love, the "Ode" was written in Havana, where he seems to have reconciled himself, once and for all, to his own sexual anomaly.

Poet in New York comes to an end with three dance poems that imply a healing of the psychic wounds described earlier in the book. The "Two Waltzes toward Civilization" bring to poetic fulfillment an aesthetic ideal that animates much of Lorca's poetry and drama, from the earliest works on: the oneness of literature and music. In his adolescent writings of 1917–18, shortly after he had abandoned the study of the piano, the poet had tried to realize this unity through the use of suggestively "musical" titles and subtitles, metaphors and images. The underlying structural principle of some of the *Suites* had been the theme and variation. By the time he wrote *Poeta en Nueva York*, a book which he regarded as "*symphonic*, like the noise and complexity" of the city itself, musical ideas had become *formative*, rather than merely decorative, elements in his writing. *Blood Wedding* (1932) is an extreme example: the contrapuntal structure of an entire scene was inspired by, and directly modeled on, the technique of "imitative entry" used by Bach in one of his cantatas.[17] Parts of the two waltzes are written in a lilting three-quarter time impossible to imitate, without loss of sense, in English: this is surely one of the most stunning experiments in "musical" literature in all of modern poetry. In "Little Viennese Waltz," the poet's darkest, most secret yearning is expressed in the lightest, most playful cadences imaginable. It is a love poem, the most explicitly homosexual one Lorca had yet written. The strains of the waltz lead the poet to a declaration of love, the gay flaunting

[16] Ibid., p. 141.
[17] See C. Maurer, "García Lorca y las formas de la música," in *Lecciones sobre Federico García Lorca*, ed. Andrés Soria Olmedo (Granada: Ediciones del Cincuentenario, 1986), pp. 235–50.

of his own beauty—"See how the hyacinths line my banks!"—
and the imagining, in the final five lines, of the consummation
of the sexual act. The ribbons of the waltz will be broken and
buried in the dark movements of the beloved.[18]

Lorca never returned to New York, and his book was not
read here until 1939–40, when the translations of Stephen Spender
and J. L. Gili were published in Britain and those of Rolfe Hum-
phries in the United States. The poet's death in Granada (1936)
was still recent, and that tragedy, and the defeat of the Republican
cause, colored the first English readings of the poems.[19] The
element of social criticism in *Poet in New York* was all but ignored
by American reviewers. Only Conrad Aiken, who later wrote
a moving "Homage to Lorca,"[20] seems to have responded to it:

There has been no more terribly acute critic of America than this steel-
conscious and death-conscious Spaniard, with his curious passion for the
modernities of nickel and tinfoil and nitre, and for the eternities of the
desert and the moon. He hated us, and rightly, for the right reasons.

V. S. Pritchett wrote: "What we call civilization, he called slime
and wire." Hardly a word was said of the poet's religious and
sexual concerns, or of his disconsolate vision of solitude and
death. One reviewer referred to Lorca's "flamboyant impressions

[18] For a discussion, see John K. Walsh, " 'Las cintas del vals': Three dance-
poems from Lorca's *Poeta en Nueva York*," *Romanic Review*, in press.
[19] The Gili/Spender and Humphries translations were reviewed by R. W.
Short, "Four Books of Poems," *Yale Review* XXX (1940), pp. 214–16; Louise
Bogan, "Books," *The New Yorker*, June 1, 1940, pp. 74–75; Muriel Rukeyser,
"Lorca in English," *Kenyon Review*, Winter 1941, pp. 123–27; Jewel Wurtz-
baugh, "F. García Lorca. *The Poet in New York*," *Books Abroad*, Spring 1941,
pp. 228–29; James A. Magner, "Poetry," *Commonweal*, Nov. 3, 1949, p. 54;
and Conrad Aiken, " 'After All, I Am a Poet,' " *New Republic*, Sept. 2, 1940,
p. 309. An excellent review of the Stephen Spender–J. L. Gili anthology is
V. S. Pritchett's "Lorca," *The New Statesman and Nation*, July 29, 1939, p. 192.
For a list of other reviews, see *OC*, Vol. III, pp. 1169–71.
[20] He titles it "The Poet in Granada." *Collected Poems* (N.Y.: Oxford Uni-
versity Press, 1953), pp. 650–58.

of New York."[21] The "myth" of his gypsiness had outlived him: he was admired in the United States as a "troubadour" and "folk poet," and more than one writer was unwilling to pardon him for having posed as a *surréaliste*. *Poet in New York* had not revealed "another" Lorca; it seemed a "jungle of disembodied surrealistic countersigns" or a book of "finger-exercises in automatic writing."[22] Even Rolfe Humphries, who translated *Poet in New York* into English for the first time, found the book "rather hysterical": in the New World, the poet "bit off more than he could chew."[23] A decade later, Roy Campbell would concur: in New York, Lorca had "lost his depth . . . his metaphors and images fall out of focus; his verse becomes loose, plaintive and slightly mephitic. It took him a long time to recover his poetical eyesight and insight . . ."[24]

Nearly fifty years after the first publication of *Poet in New York*, a far different opinion prevails. No one would argue now that the book is a stylistic "exercise." Lorca's strange poetic idiom is now seen to answer to a dark, and deadly serious, vision of human life, one whose mystery will trouble a new generation of readers. The years have broadened the meaning of the poems. The title has all but lost its paradox and the evils of the city seem no more characteristic of Manhattan than of Madrid or, for that matter, of Granada. The "gypsy poet" has disappeared, but Lorca's cry of anguish and vision of human solitude seem destined to endure.

Christopher Maurer

Cambridge, Massachusetts
June 1987

[21] Magner, p. 54.

[22] Short, p. 215.

[23] Daniel Eisenberg, *Poeta en Nueva York: historia y problemas de un texto de Lorca* (Barcelona: Ariel, 1976), p. 58. I have translated from the Spanish text.

[24] Roy Campbell, *Lorca: An Appreciation of His Poetry* (New Haven: Yale University Press, 1952), pp. 94–95.

Poet in New York / Poeta en Nueva York

A Bebé y Carlos Morla

*Los poemas de este libro están escritos en
la ciudad de Nueva York, el año
1929–1930, en que el poeta vivió como
estudiante en Columbia University.*

[F.G.L.]

To Bebé and Carlos Morla

*The poems in this book were written
in New York City in 1929–30, while
the poet was living as a student at
Columbia University.*
                    [F.G.L.]

I
POEMAS DE
LA SOLEDAD
EN COLUMBIA
UNIVERSITY

Furia color de amor,
amor color de olvido.
—LUIS CERNUDA

I

POEMS OF

SOLITUDE

AT COLUMBIA

UNIVERSITY

Rage, love's color,
love, the color of oblivion.
—LUIS CERNUDA

[Lorca at Columbia, October 1929]

Vuelta de paseo

Asesinado por el cielo.
Entre las formas que van hacia la sierpe
y las formas que buscan el cristal
dejaré crecer mis cabellos.

Con el árbol de muñones que no canta
y el niño con el blanco rostro de huevo.

Con los animalitos de cabeza rota
y el agua harapienta de los pies secos.

Con todo lo que tiene cansancio sordomudo
y mariposa ahogada en el tintero.

Tropezando con mi rostro distinto de cada día.
¡Asesinado por el cielo!

After a Walk

Cut down by the sky.
Between shapes moving toward the serpent
and crystal-craving shapes,
I'll let my hair grow.

With the amputated tree that doesn't sing
and the child with the blank face of an egg.

With the little animals whose skulls are cracked
and the water, dressed in rags, but with dry feet.

With all the bone-tired, deaf-and-dumb things
and a butterfly drowned in the inkwell.

Bumping into my own face, different each day.
Cut down by the sky!

1910
(Intermedio)

Aquellos ojos míos de mil novecientos diez
no vieron enterrar a los muertos,
ni la feria de ceniza del que llora por la madrugada,
ni el corazón que tiembla arrinconado como un caballito
    de mar.

Aquellos ojos míos de mil novecientos diez
vieron la blanca pared donde orinaban las niñas,
el hocico del toro, la seta venenosa
y una luna incomprensible que iluminaba por los
    rincones
los pedazos de limón seco bajo el negro duro de las
    botellas.

Aquellos ojos míos en el cuello de la jaca,
en el seno traspasado de Santa Rosa dormida,
en los tejados del amor, con gemidos y frescas manos,
en un jardín donde los gatos se comían a las ranas.

Desván donde el polvo viejo congrega estatuas y
    musgos.
Cajas que guardan silencio de cangrejos devorados.
En el sitio donde el sueño tropezaba con su realidad.
Allí mis pequeños ojos.

No preguntarme nada. He visto que las cosas
cuando buscan su curso encuentran su vacío.
Hay un dolor de huecos por el aire sin gente
y en mis ojos criaturas vestidas ¡sin desnudo!

Nueva York, agosto 1929

1910
(Intermezzo)

Those eyes of mine in nineteen-ten
saw no one dead and buried,
no village fair of ash from the one who weeps at dawn,
no trembling heart cornered like a sea horse.

Those eyes of mine in nineteen-ten
saw the white wall where little girls pissed,
the bull's muzzle, the poisonous mushroom,
and an incomprehensible moon illuminating dried lemon
   rinds
under the hard black bottles in corners.

Those eyes of mine on the pony's neck,
on the pierced breast of Santa Rosa as she sleeps,
on the rooftops of love, with moans and cool hands,
on a garden where cats devour frogs.

Attic where the ancient dust assembles statues and moss.
Boxes that keep the silence of devoured crabs.
In the place where the dream was colliding with its
   reality.
My little eyes are there.

Don't ask me any questions. I've seen how things
that seek their way find their void instead.
There are spaces that ache in the uninhabited air
and in my eyes, completely dressed creatures—no one
   naked there!

New York, August 1929

9.

La aurora

La aurora de Nueva York tiene
cuatro columnas de cieno
y un huracán de negras palomas
que chapotean las aguas podridas.

La aurora de Nueva York gime
por las inmensas escaleras
buscando entre las aristas
nardos de angustia dibujada.

La aurora llega y nadie la recibe en su boca
porque allí no hay mañana ni esperanza posible:
a veces las monedas en enjambres furiosos
taladran y devoran abandonados niños.

Los primeros que salen comprenden con sus huesos
que no habrá paraíso ni amores deshojados:
saben que van al cieno de números y leyes,
a los juegos sin arte, a sudores sin fruto.

La luz es sepultada por cadenas y ruidos
en impúdico reto de ciencia sin raíces.
Por los barrios hay gentes que vacilan insomnes
como recién salidas de un naufragio de sangre.

Dawn

Dawn in New York has
four columns of mire
and a hurricane of black pigeons
splashing in the putrid waters.

Dawn in New York groans
on enormous fire escapes
searching between the angles
for spikenards of drafted anguish.

Dawn arrives and no one receives it in his mouth
because morning and hope are impossible there:
sometimes the furious swarming coins
penetrate like drills and devour abandoned children.

Those who go out early know in their bones
there will be no paradise or loves that bloom and die:
they know they will be mired in numbers and laws,
in mindless games, in fruitless labors.

The light is buried under chains and noises
in an impudent challenge to rootless science.
And crowds stagger sleeplessly through the boroughs
as if they had just escaped a shipwreck of blood.

Tu infancia en Menton

Sí, tu niñez: ya fábula de fuentes.

—JORGE GUILLÉN

Sí, tu niñez: ya fábula de fuentes.
El tren y la mujer que llena el cielo.
Tu soledad esquiva en los hoteles
y tu máscara pura de otro signo.
Es la niñez del mar y tu silencio
donde los sabios vidrios se quebraban.
Es tu yerta ignorancia donde estuvo
mi torso limitado por el fuego.
Norma de amor te di, hombre de Apolo,
llanto con ruiseñor enajenado,
pero, pasto de ruina, te afilabas
para los breves sueños indecisos.
Pensamiento de enfrente, luz de ayer,
índices y señales del acaso.
Tu cintura de arena sin sosiego
atiende sólo rastros que no escalan.
Pero yo he de buscar por los rincones
tu alma tibia sin ti que no te entiende,
con el dolor de Apolo detenido
con que he roto la máscara que llevas.
Allí, león, allí, furia de cielo,
te dejaré pacer en mis mejillas;
allí, caballo azul de mi locura,
pulso de nebulosa y minutero.
He de buscar las piedras de alacranes
y los vestidos de tu madre niña,
llanto de media noche y paño roto

Your Childhood in Menton

Yes, your childhood: now a fable of fountains.

—JORGE GUILLÉN

Yes, your childhood: now a fable of fountains.
The train and the woman who fills the sky.
Your shy loneliness in hotels
and your pure mask of another sign.
The sea's childhood and your silence
where the crystals of wisdom shattered.
Your rigid ignorance where
my torso was circumscribed by fire.
What I gave you, Apollonian man, was the standard of
  love,
fits of tears with an estranged nightingale.
But ruin fed upon you, you whittled yourself to nothing
for the sake of fleeting, aimless dreams.
Thoughts before you, yesterday's light,
traces and signs of what might be . . .
Your waist of restless sand
follows only trails that do not climb.
But in every corner I must look for your warm soul
that is without you and doesn't understand you,
with the sorrow of Apollo stopped in his tracks,
the sorrow with which I shattered your mask.
It's there, lion, there, sky's fury,
where I'll let you graze on my cheeks;
there, blue horse of my insanity,
pulse of the nebula and hand that counts the minutes.
There I'll look for the scorpions' stones
and the clothes of the girl who was your mother,
midnight tears and torn cloth

que quitó luna de la sien del muerto.
Sí, tu niñez: ya fábula de fuentes.
Alma extraña de mi hueco de venas,
te he de buscar pequeña y sin raíces.
¡Amor de siempre, amor, amor de nunca!
¡Oh, sí! Yo quiero. ¡Amor, amor! Dejadme.
No me tapen la boca los que buscan
espigas de Saturno por la nieve
o castran animales por un cielo,
clínica y selva de la anatomía.
Amor, amor, amor. Niñez del mar.
Tu alma tibia sin ti que no te entiende.
Amor, amor, un vuelo de la corza
por el pecho sin fin de la blancura.
Y tu niñez, amor, y tu niñez.
El tren y la mujer que llena el cielo.
Ni tú, ni yo, ni el aire, ni las hojas.
Sí, tu niñez: ya fábula de fuentes.

that wiped moonlight from the temples of the dead
  man.
Yes, your childhood: now a fable of fountains.
Strange soul, tiny and adrift, ripped
from the emptied space of my veins—I must look until I
  find you.
The same love as ever, but never the same!
Yes, I do love! Love! Leave me alone, all of you.
And don't try to cover my mouth, you who seek
the wheat of Saturn in snowfields,
or castrate animals on behalf of a sky,
anatomy's clinic and jungle.
Love, love, love. The sea's childhood.
Your warm soul that is without you and doesn't
  understand you.
Love, love, the flight of the doe
through the endless breast of whiteness.
And your childhood, love, your childhood.
The train and the woman who fills the sky.
Not you, not me, not the air, not the leaves.
Yes, your childhood: now a fable of fountains.

Fábula y rueda de los tres amigos

Enrique,
Emilio,
Lorenzo.
Estaban los tres helados:
Enrique por el mundo de las camas,
Emilio por el mundo de los ojos y las heridas de las
   manos,
Lorenzo por el mundo de las universidades sin tejados.

Lorenzo,
Emilio,
Enrique.
Estaban los tres quemados:
Lorenzo por el mundo de las hojas y las bolas de billar,
Emilio por el mundo de la sangre y los alfileres blancos,
Enrique por el mundo de los muertos y los periódicos
   abandonados.

Lorenzo,
Emilio,
Enrique.
Estaban los tres enterrados:
Lorenzo en un seno de Flora,
Emilio en la yerta ginebra que se olvida en el vaso,
Enrique en la hormiga, en el mar y en los ojos vacíos de
   los pájaros.

Lorenzo,
Emilio,
Enrique.
Fueron los tres en mis manos

16.

Fable of Three Friends to Be Sung in Rounds

Enrique,
Emilio,
Lorenzo.
The three of them were frozen:
Enrique in the world of beds,
Emilio in the world of eyes and wounded hands,
Lorenzo in the world of roofless universities.

Lorenzo,
Emilio,
Enrique.
The three of them were burned:
Lorenzo in the world of leaves and billiard balls,
Emilio in the world of blood and white pins,
Enrique in the world of the dead and discarded
    newspapers.

Lorenzo,
Emilio,
Enrique.
The three of them were buried:
Lorenzo in Flora's breast,
Emilio in the forgotten shot of gin,
Enrique in the ant, the sea, the empty eyes of the birds.

Lorenzo,
Emilio,
Enrique.
In my hands the three of them were

tres montañas chinas,
tres sombras de caballo,
tres paisajes de nieve y una cabaña de azucenas
por los palomares donde la luna se pone plana bajo el
  gallo.

Uno
y uno
y uno.
Estaban los tres momificados,
con las moscas del invierno,
con los tinteros que orina el perro y desprecia el vilano,
con la brisa que hiela el corazón de todas las madres,
por los blancos derribos de Júpiter donde meriendan
  muerte los borrachos.

Tres
y dos
y uno.
Los vi perderse llorando y cantando
por un huevo de gallina,
por la noche que enseñaba su esqueleto de tabaco,
por mi dolor lleno de rostros y punzantes esquirlas de
  luna
por mi alegría de ruedas dentadas y látigos,
por mi pecho turbado por las palomas,
por mi muerte desierta con un solo paseante equivocado.

Yo había matado la quinta luna
y bebían agua por las fuentes los abanicos y los aplausos.
Tibia leche encerrada de las recién paridas
agitaba las rosas con un largo dolor blanco.

three Chinese mountains,
three shadows of horses,
three snowy landscapes and a shelter of lilies
by the dovecotes where the moon lies flat beneath the
    rooster.

One
and one
and one.
The three of them were mummified
with winter flies,
with the inkwells that dogs piss and thistledown
    despises,
with the breeze that chills every mother's heart,
by Jupiter's white wreckage, where the drunks lunch on
    death.

Three
and two
and one.
I saw them ruin themselves, weeping and singing,
in a hen's egg,
in the night that showed its tobacco skeleton,
in my sorrow, full of faces and piercing lunar shrapnel,
in my joy of serrated wheels and whips,
in my breast that is troubled with doves,
in my deserted death with a lone mistaken passerby.

I had killed the fifth moon,
and the fans and applause were drinking water from the
    fountains.
Warm milk inside the new mothers
was stirring the roses with a long white sorrow.

19.

Enrique,
Emilio,
Lorenzo.
Diana es dura,
pero a veces tiene los pechos nublados.
Puede la piedra blanca latir en la sangre del ciervo
y el ciervo puede soñar por los ojos de un caballo.

Cuando se hundieron las formas puras
bajo el cri cri de las margaritas,
comprendí que me habían asesinado.
Recorrieron los cafés y los cementerios y las iglesias.
Abrieron los toneles y los armarios.
Destrozaron tres esqueletos para arrancar sus dientes de
    oro.
Ya no me encontraron.
¿No me encontraron?
No. No me encontraron.
Pero se supo que la sexta luna huyó torrente arriba,
y que el mar recordó ¡de pronto!
los nombres de todos sus ahogados.

20.

Enrique,
Emilio,
Lorenzo.
Diana is hard,
but sometimes her breasts are banked with clouds.
The white stone can throb in deer blood
and the deer can dream through the eyes of a horse.

When the pure shapes sank
under the chirping of daisies,
I knew they had murdered me.
They combed the cafés, graveyards, and churches for
    me,
pried open casks and cabinets,
destroyed three skeletons in order to rip out their gold
    teeth.
But they couldn't find me anymore.
They couldn't?
No, they couldn't find me.
But they discovered the sixth moon had fled against the
    torrent,
and the sea—suddenly!—remembered
the names of all its drowned.

II

LOS NEGROS

Para Ángel del Río

II

THE BLACKS

For Ángel del Río

[García Lorca, *Vase on a Tile Roof*,
New York, 1929]

Norma y paraíso de los negros

Odian la sombra del pájaro
sobre el pleamar de la blanca mejilla
y el conflicto de luz y viento
en el salón de la nieve fría.

Odian la flecha sin cuerpo,
el pañuelo exacto de la despedida,
la aguja que mantiene presión y rosa
en el gramíneo rubor de la sonrisa.

Aman el azul desierto,
las vacilantes expresiones bovinas,
la mentirosa luna de los polos,
la danza curva del agua en la orilla.

Con la ciencia del tronco y el rastro
llenan de nervios luminosos la arcilla
y patinan lúbricos por aguas y arenas
gustando la amarga frescura de su milenaria saliva.

Es por el azul crujiente,
azul sin un gusano ni una huella dormida,
donde los huevos de avestruz quedan eternos
y deambulan intactas las lluvias bailarinas.

Es por el azul sin historia,
azul de una noche sin temor de día,
azul donde el desnudo del viento va quebrando
los camellos sonámbulos de las nubes vacías.

Standards and Paradise of the Blacks

They hate the bird's shadow
on the white cheek's high tide
and the conflict of light and wind
in the great cold hall of snow.

They hate the unbodied arrow,
the punctual handkerchief of farewell,
the needle that pressures redness
into their smiles as green as the grass.

They love the deserted blue,
the swaying bovine faces,
the deceitful moon of both poles,
and water's bent dance on the shoreline.

They use the science of tree trunk and rake
to cover the clay with luminous nerves,
and as they skate, gliding over water and sand,
they taste the bitter freshness of their millenary spit.

It's in the crackling blue,
blue without a single worm or sleeping footprint,
where the ostrich eggs stay forever
and the untouched rains dance and stroll.

It's in the blue that has no history,
blue of a night without fear of day,
blue where the naked body of the wind goes to break up
camels of empty clouds moving in their sleep.

Es allí donde sueñan los torsos bajo la gula de la hierba.
Allí los corales empapan la desesperación de la tinta,
los durmientes borran sus perfiles bajo la madeja de los
 caracoles
y queda el hueco de la danza sobre las últimas cenizas.

It's there the torsos dream beneath the hungry grass,
there the coral absorbs the ink's desperation,
the sleepers erase their profiles under the skein of snails,
and the emptied space of the dance stays above the last
   of the ashes.

El rey de Harlem

Con una cuchara de palo
le arrancaba los ojos a los cocodrilos
y golpeaba el trasero de los monos.
Con una cuchara de palo.

Fuego de siempre dormía en los pedernales
y los escarabajos borrachos de anís
olvidaban el musgo de las aldeas.

Aquel viejo cubierto de setas
iba al sitio donde lloraban los negros
mientras crujía la cuchara del rey
y llegaban los tanques de agua podrida.

Las rosas huían por los filos
de las últimas curvas del aire
y en los montones de azafrán
los niños machacaban pequeñas ardillas
con un rubor de frenesí manchado.

Es preciso cruzar los puentes
y llegar al rumor negro
para que el perfume de pulmón
nos golpee las sienes con su vestido
de caliente piña.

Es preciso matar al rubio vendedor de aguardiente,
a todos los amigos de la manzana y la arena;
y es necesario dar con los puños cerrados
a las pequeñas judías que tiemblan llenas de burbujas,

The King of Harlem

With a wooden spoon
he dug out the crocodiles' eyes,
and swatted the monkeys on their asses.
With a wooden spoon.

Age–old fire slept in the flints
and the beetles drunk on anisette
forgot about the moss of the villages.

The old man covered with mushrooms
was on his way to the place where the blacks wept
while the king's spoon cracked
and the vats of putrid water arrived.

The roses fled along the blades
of the air's last curves,
and on the piles of saffron
the children flattened tiny squirrels
with faces flushed in their strained frenzy.

It's necessary to cross the bridges
and reach the murmuring blacks
so the perfume of their lungs
can buffet our temples with its covering
of hot pineapple.

It's necessary to kill the blond vendor of firewater
and every friend of apple and sand,
and it's necessary to use the fists
against the little Jewish women who tremble, filled with
    bubbles,

29.

para que el rey de Harlem cante con su muchedumbre,
para que los cocodrilos duerman en largas filas
bajo el amianto de la luna,
y para que nadie dude la infinita belleza
de los plumeros, los ralladores, los cobres y las cacerolas
   de las cocinas.

¡Ay, Harlem! ¡Ay, Harlem! ¡Ay, Harlem!
No hay angustia comparable a tus rojos oprimidos,
a tu sangre estremecida dentro del eclipse oscuro,
a tu violencia granate, sordomuda en la penumbra,
a tu gran rey prisionero, con un traje de conserje.

          .   .   .

Tenía la noche una hendidura y quietas salamandras de
   marfil.
Las muchachas americanas
llevaban niños y monedas en el vientre
y los muchachos se desmayaban en la cruz del
   desperezo.

Ellos son.
Ellos son los que beben el whisky de plata junto a los
   volcanes
y tragan pedacitos de corazón por las heladas montañas
   del oso.

Aquella noche el rey de Harlem, con una durísima
   cuchara,
le arrancaba los ojos a los cocodrilos
y golpeaba el trasero de los monos.
Con una durísima cuchara.

so the king of Harlem sings with his multitude,
so crocodiles sleep in long rows
beneath the moon's asbestos,
and so no one doubts the infinite beauty
of feather dusters, graters, copper pans, and kitchen
    casseroles.

Ay, Harlem! *Ay*, Harlem! *Ay*, Harlem!
There is no anguish like that of your oppressed reds,
or your blood shuddering with rage inside the dark
    eclipse,
or your garnet violence, deaf and dumb in the
    penumbra,
or your grand king a prisoner in the uniform of a
    doorman.

·   ·   ·

The night was cracked, and there were motionless ivory
    salamanders.
American girls
were carrying babies and coins in their wombs,
and the boys stretched their limbs and fainted on the
    cross.

They are the ones.
The ones who drink silver whisky near the volcanoes
and swallow pieces of heart by the bear's frozen
    mountains.

That night the king of Harlem, with an unbreakable
    spoon,
dug out the crocodiles' eyes
and swatted the monkeys on their asses.
With an unbreakable spoon.

31.

Los negros lloraban confundidos
entre paraguas y soles de oro,
los mulatos estiraban gomas, ansiosos de llegar al torso
    blanco,
y el viento empañaba espejos
y quebraba las venas de los bailarines.

¡Negros! ¡Negros! ¡Negros! ¡Negros!
La sangre no tiene puertas en vuestra noche boca arriba.
No hay rubor. Sangre furiosa por debajo de las pieles,
viva en la espina del puñal y en el pecho de los paisajes,
bajo las pinzas y las retamas de la celeste luna de Cáncer.

Sangre que busca por mil caminos muertes enharinadas
    y ceniza de nardos,
cielos yertos en declive donde las colonias de planetas
rueden por las playas con los objetos abandonados.

Sangre que mira lenta con el rabo del ojo,
hecha de espartos exprimidos y néctares subterráneos.
Sangre que oxida al alisio descuidado en una huella
y disuelve a las mariposas en los cristales de la ventana.

Es la sangre que viene, que vendrá
por los tejados y azoteas, por todas partes,
para quemar la clorofila de las mujeres rubias,
para gemir al pie de las camas, ante el insomnio de los
    lavabos,
y estrellarse en una aurora de tabaco y bajo amarillo.

¡Hay que huir!,
huir por las esquinas y encerrarse en los últimos pisos,

The blacks cried in confusion
among umbrellas and gold suns,
the mulattoes stretched rubber, thinking anxiously of
    turning their torsos white,
and the wind tarnished mirrors
and shattered the veins of the dancers.

Blacks! Blacks! Blacks! Blacks!
The blood has no doors in your recumbent night.
No blush in your face. Blood rages beneath skin,
alive in the dagger's spine and the landscapes' breast,
under the pincers and Scotch broom of Cancer's
    heavenly moon.

Blood that searches a thousand roads for deaths dusted
    with flour and ashes of spikenards,
rigid, descending skies in which the colonies of planets
can wheel with the litter on the beaches.

Blood that looks slowly from the corner of an eye,
blood wrung from hemp and subway nectars.
Blood that rusts the careless trade wind in a footprint
and dissolves butterflies in windowpanes.

Blood flows, and will flow
on rooftops everywhere,
and burn the blond women's chlorophyll,
and groan at the foot of the beds near the washstands'
    insomnia,
and burst into an aurora of tobacco and low yellow.

There must be some way out of here,
some street to flee down, some locked room on the top
    floor to hide in,

33.

porque el tuétano del bosque penetrará por las rendijas
para dejar en vuestra carne una leve huella de eclipse
y una falsa tristeza de guante desteñido y rosa química.

. . .

Es por el silencio sapientísimo
cuando los cocineros y los camareros y los que limpian
 con la lengua
las heridas de los millonarios
buscan al rey por las calles o en los ángulos del salitre.

Un viento sur de madera, oblicuo en el negro fango,
escupe a las barcas rotas y se clava puntillas en los
 hombros.
Un viento sur que lleva
colmillos, girasoles, alfabetos
y una pila de Volta con avispas ahogadas.

El olvido estaba expresado por tres gotas de tinta sobre
 el monóculo.
El amor, por un solo rostro invisible a flor de piedra.
Médulas y corolas componían sobre las nubes
un desierto de tallos, sin una sola rosa.

A la izquierda, a la derecha, por el Sur y por el Norte,
se levanta el muro impasible
para el topo y la aguja del agua.
No busquéis, negros, su grieta
para hallar la máscara infinita.
Buscad el gran sol del centro
hechos una piña zumbadora.
El sol que se desliza por los bosques
seguro de no encontrar una ninfa.

because the forest's marrow will slip through the cracks
to leave on your skin a faint trace of an eclipse
and a false sorrow of faded glove and chemical rose.

. . .

Through the all-knowing silence,
cooks, waiters, and those whose tongues lick clean
the wounds of millionaires
seek the king in the streets or on the sharp angles of
    saltpeter.

A wooden wind from the south, slanting through the
    black mire,
spits on the broken boats and drives tacks into
    shoulders.
A south wind that carries
tusks, sunflowers, alphabets,
and a battery with drowned wasps.

Oblivion was expressed by three drops of ink on the
    monocle.
Love, by a single, invisible, stone-deep face.
And above the clouds, bone marrow and corollas
composed a desert of stems without a single rose.

To the left and right, south and north,
the wall rises, impassable
for the mole and the needle made of water.
Blacks, don't look in its cracks
to find the infinite mask.
Look for the great central sun.
Turn into a swarm of buzzing pineapple.
The sun that slides through the forests,
sure that a nymph will not be there.

35.

El sol que destruye números y no ha cruzado nunca un
    sueño,
el tatuado sol que baja por el río
y muge seguido de caimanes.

¡Negros! ¡Negros! ¡Negros! ¡Negros!
Jamás sierpe, ni cebra, ni mula
palidecieron al morir.
El leñador no sabe cuándo expiran
los clamorosos árboles que corta.
Aguardad bajo la sombra vegetal de vuestro rey
a que cicutas y cardos y ortigas turben postreras azoteas.

Entonces, negros, entonces, entonces,
podréis besar con frenesí las ruedas de las bicicletas,
poner parejas de microscopios en las cuevas de las
    ardillas
y danzar al fin sin duda, mientras las flores erizadas
asesinan a nuestro Moisés casi en los juncos del cielo.

¡Ay, Harlem disfrazada!
¡Ay, Harlem, amenazada por un gentío de trajes sin
    cabeza!
Me llega tu rumor,
me llega tu rumor atravesando troncos y ascensores,
a través de láminas grises,
donde flotan tus automóviles cubiertos de dientes,
a través de los caballos muertos y los crímenes
    diminutos,
a través de tu gran rey desesperado,
cuyas barbas llegan al mar.

The sun that destroys numbers, and has never crossed a
    dream,
the tattooed sun that descends the river
and bellows just ahead of the crocodiles.

Blacks! Blacks! Blacks! Blacks!
No serpent, no zebra or mule
ever turned pale in the face of death.
The woodcutter doesn't know when the clamorous trees
that he cuts down expire.
Wait in your king's jungle shade
until hemlock, thistles, and nettles disturb the last
    rooftops.

Then, blacks, and only then
will you be able to frantically kiss bicycle wheels,
place pairs of microscopes in squirrel lairs,
and dance fearlessly at last while the bristling flowers
cut down our Moses in the bulrushes that border
    heaven.

Ay, Harlem in disguise!
Ay, Harlem, threatened by a mob of headless suits!
I hear your murmur,
I hear it moving through tree trunks and elevator shafts,
through gray sheets
where your cars float covered with teeth,
through dead horses and petty crimes,
through your grand, despairing king
whose beard reaches the sea.

Iglesia abandonada
(Balada de la Gran Guerra)

Yo tenía un hijo que se llamaba Juan.
Yo tenía un hijo.
Se perdió por los arcos un viernes de todos los muertos.
Lo vi jugar en las últimas escaleras de la misa
y echaba un cubito de hojalata en el corazón del
    sacerdote.
He golpeado los ataúdes. ¡Mi hijo! ¡Mi hijo! ¡Mi hijo!
Saqué una pata de gallina por detrás de la luna y luego
comprendí que mi niña era un pez
por donde se alejan las carretas.
Yo tenía una niña.
Yo tenía un pez muerto bajo la ceniza de los incensarios.
Yo tenía un mar. ¿De qué? ¡Dios mío! ¡Un mar!
Subí a tocar las campanas, pero las frutas tenían gusanos
y las cerillas apagadas
se comían los trigos de la primavera.
Yo vi la transparente cigüeña de alcohol
mondar las negras cabezas de los soldados agonizantes
y vi las cabañas de goma
donde giraban las copas llenas de lágrimas.
En las anémonas del ofertorio te encontraré, ¡corazón
    mío!,
cuando el sacerdote levante la mula y el buey con sus
    fuertes brazos,
para espantar los sapos nocturnos que rondan los helados
    paisajes del cáliz.
Yo tenía un hijo que era un gigante,
pero los muertos son más fuertes y saben devorar
    pedazos de cielo.
Si mi niño hubiera sido un oso,

Abandoned Church
(Ballad of the Great War)

Once I had a son named John.
Once I had a son.
He was lost in the arches, one Friday, Day of the Dead.
I saw him playing on the last raised steps of the Mass
and he lowered a tin bucket into the priest's deep heart.
I pounded on the coffins. My son! My son! My son!
I pulled a chicken leg from behind the moon and
    suddenly
realized that my girl had become a fish
where carts recede in the distance.
Once I had a little girl.
Once I had a dead fish beneath the ashes of the censers.
Once I had a sea. Of what? My God! A sea!
I climbed up to ring the bells, but the fruit was wormy
and the snuffed-out tapers
had eaten the spring wheat.
I saw the transparent stork of alcohol
picking clean the black heads of dying soldiers
and I saw the shelters of rubber
where the spinning cups brimmed with tears.
I'll find you, my dear son, in anemones of the offertory
when the priest lifts the mule and the ox with his
    powerful arms,
to frighten nocturnal toads that roam the chalice's frozen
    landscape.
Once I had a son who was a giant,
but the dead are more powerful and can devour pieces
    of the sky.
If my boy had been a bear,

39.

yo no temería el sigilo de los caimanes,
ni hubiese visto el mar amarrado a los árboles
para ser fornicado y herido por el tropel de los
   regimientos.
¡Si mi niño hubiera sido un oso!
Me envolveré sobre esta lona dura para no sentir el frío
   de los musgos.
Sé muy bien que me darán una manga o la corbata;
pero en el centro de la misa yo romperé el timón y
   entonces
vendrá a la piedra la locura de pingüinos y gaviotas
que harán decir a los que duermen y a los que cantan
   por las esquinas:
Él tenía un hijo.
¡Un hijo! ¡Un hijo! ¡Un hijo
que no era más que suyo, porque era su hijo!
¡Su hijo! ¡Su hijo! ¡Su hijo!

I wouldn't fear the crocodiles lying in ambush,
or have seen the sea lashed to the trees
for the brutal pleasure of the regiments.
If only my boy had been a bear!
I'll lie down and wrap myself in this rough canvas so I
    won't feel the cold moss.
I know very well that I'll be given shirt sleeves or a tie;
but in the middle of Mass I'll break the rudder and then
the insanity of penguins and gulls will come to the stone
and make those who sleep and sing on street corners
    say:
Once he had a son.
A son! A son! A son
who was his alone, because he was his son!
His son! His son! His son!

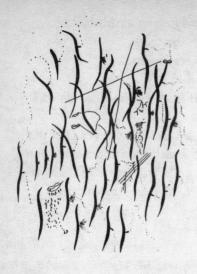

III

CALLES

Y SUEÑOS

A Rafael R. Rapún

Un pájaro de papel en el pecho
dice que el tiempo de los besos no ha llegado.
—VICENTE ALEIXANDRE

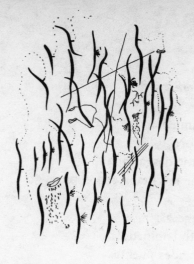

III

STREETS

AND DREAMS

To Rafael R. Rapún

A paper bird inside the breast
Says the time for kisses is still not here.
—VICENTE ALEIXANDRE

[García Lorca, *Sexual Forest*, 1933]

Danza de la muerte

El mascarón. Mirad el mascarón
cómo viene del África a New York.

Se fueron los árboles de la pimienta,
los pequeños botones de fósforo.
Se fueron los camellos de carne desgarrada
y los valles de luz que el cisne levantaba con el pico.

Era el momento de las cosas secas:
de la espiga en el ojo y el gato laminado;
del óxido de hierro de los grandes puentes
y el definitivo silencio del corcho.

Era la gran reunión de los animales muertos
traspasados por las espadas de la luz.
La alegría eterna del hipopótamo con las pezuñas de
    ceniza
y de la gacela con una siempreviva en la garganta.

En la marchita soledad sin onda
el abollado mascarón danzaba.
Medio lado del mundo era de arena,
mercurio y sol dormido el otro medio.

El mascarón. ¡Mirad el mascarón!
Arena, caimán y miedo sobre Nueva York.

Desfiladeros de cal aprisionaban un cielo vacío
donde sonaban las voces de los que mueren bajo el
    guano.

Dance of Death

The mask. Look how the mask
comes from Africa to New York.

They are gone, the pepper trees,
the tiny buds of phosphorus.
They are gone, the camels with torn flesh,
and the valleys of light the swan lifted in its beak.

It was the time of parched things,
the wheat spear in the eye, the laminated cat,
the time of tremendous, rusting bridges
and the deathly silence of cork.

It was the great gathering of dead animals
pierced by the swords of light.
The endless joy of the hippopotamus with cloven feet of
    ash
and of the gazelle with an immortelle in its throat.

In the withered, waveless solitude,
the dented mask was dancing.
Half of the world was sand,
the other half mercury and dormant sunlight.

The mask. Look at the mask!
Sand, crocodile, and fear above New York.

Canyons of lime imprisoned an empty sky,
where the voices of those who die under the guano were
    heard.

Un cielo mondado y puro, idéntico a sí mismo,
con el bozo y lirio agudo de sus montañas invisibles,

acabó con los más leves tallitos del canto
y se fue al diluvio empaquetado de la savia,
a través del descanso de los últimos perfiles
levantando con el rabo pedazos de espejo.

Cuando el chino lloraba en el tejado
sin encontrar el desnudo de su mujer,
y el director del banco observaba el manómetro
que mide el cruel silencio de la moneda,
el mascarón llegaba a Wall Street.

No es extraño para la danza
este columbario que pone los ojos amarillos.
De la esfinge a la caja de caudales hay un hilo tenso
que atraviesa el corazón de todos los niños pobres.
El ímpetu primitivo baila con el ímpetu mecánico,
ignorantes en su frenesí de la luz original.
Porque si la rueda olvida su fórmula,
ya puede cantar desnuda con las manadas de caballos;
y si una llama quema los helados proyectos
el cielo tendrá que huir ante el tumulto de las ventanas.

No es extraño este sitio para la danza. Yo lo digo.
El mascarón bailará entre columnas de sangre y de
    números,
entre huracanes de oro y gemidos de obreros parados
que aullarán, noche oscura, por tu tiempo sin luces.

A pure and manicured sky, identical with itself,
with the down and the keen-edged iris of its invisible
  mountains—

it finished off the slender stems of song
and was swept away toward channels of sap,
through the stillness of the last profiles,
lifting pieces of mirror with its tail.

While the Chinaman wept on the roof
without finding the naked body of his wife,
and the bank director examined the manometer
that measures the cruel silence of money,
the mask arrived on Wall Street.

It isn't a strange place for the dance,
these cemetery niches that turn the eyes yellow.
Between the sphinx and the bank vault, there is a taut
  thread
that pierces the heart of all poor children.
The primitive impetus dances with the mechanical
  impetus,
unaware, in their frenzy, of the original light.
Because if the wheel forgets its formula,
it will sing naked with herds of horses;
and if a flame burns the frozen blueprints,
the sky will have to flee before the tumult of windows.

This isn't a strange place for the dance, I tell you.
The mask will dance among columns of blood and
  numbers,
among hurricanes of gold and groans of the
  unemployed,
who will howl, in the dead of night, for your dark time.

47.

¡Oh salvaje Norteamérica!, ¡oh impúdica!, ¡oh salvaje!
Tendida en la frontera de la nieve.

El mascarón. ¡Mirad el mascarón!
¡Qué ola de fango y luciérnagas sobre Nueva York!

· · ·

Yo estaba en la terraza luchando con la luna.
Enjambres de ventanas acribillaban un muslo de la
    noche.
En mis ojos bebían las dulces vacas de los cielos
y las brisas de largos remos
golpeaban los cenicientos cristales del Broadway.

La gota de sangre buscaba la luz de la yema del astro
para fingir una muerta semilla de manzana.
El aire de la llanura, empujado por los pastores,
temblaba con un miedo de molusco sin concha.

Pero no son los muertos los que bailan.
Estoy seguro.
Los muertos están embebidos devorando sus propias
    manos.
Son los otros los que bailan con el mascarón y su
    vihuela.
Son los otros, los borrachos de plata, los hombres fríos,
los que duermen en el cruce de los muslos y llamas
    duras,
los que buscan la lombriz en el paisaje de las escaleras,
los que beben en el banco lágrimas de niña muerta
o los que comen por las esquinas diminutas pirámides
    del alba.

Oh, savage, shameless North America!
Stretched out on the frontier of snow.

The mask. Look at the mask!
Such a wave of mire and fireflies above New York!

. . .

I was on the terrace, wrestling with the moon.
Swarms of windows riddled one of the night's thighs.
Placid sky-cattle drank from my eyes
and the breezes on long oars
struck the ashen store windows on Broadway.

The drop of blood looked for light in the star's yolk
so as to seem a dead apple seed.
The prairie air, driven by the shepherds,
trembled in fear like a mollusk without its shell.

But I'm sure there are no dancers
among the dead.
The dead are engrossed in devouring their own hands.
It's the others who dance with the mask and its *vihuela*.
Others, drunk on silver, cold men,
who sleep where thighs and hard flames intersect,
who seek the earthworm in the landscape of fire escapes,
who drink a dead girl's tears at the bank
or eat pyramids of dawn on tiny street corners.

¡Que no baile el Papa!
¡No, que no baile el Papa!
Ni el Rey,
ni el millonario de dientes azules,
ni las bailarinas secas de las catedrales,
ni constructores, ni esmeraldas, ni locos, ni sodomitas.
Sólo este mascarón.
Este mascarón de vieja escarlatina.
¡Sólo este mascarón!

Que ya las cobras silbarán por los últimos pisos.
Que ya las ortigas estremecerán patios y terrazas.
Que ya la Bolsa será una pirámide de musgo.
Que ya vendrán lianas después de los fusiles
y muy pronto, muy pronto, muy pronto.
¡Ay, Wall Street!

El mascarón. ¡Mirad el mascarón!
¡Cómo escupe veneno de bosque
por la angustia imperfecta de Nueva York!

Diciembre 1929

But don't let the Pope dance!
No, don't let the Pope dance!
Nor the King,
nor the millionaires with blue teeth,
nor the barren dancers of the cathedrals,
nor builders, nor emeralds, nor madmen, nor
    sodomites.
Only this mask.
This mask of ancient scarlet fever.
Only this mask!

Cobras shall hiss on the top floors.
Nettles shall shake courtyards and terraces.
The Stock Exchange shall become a pyramid of moss.
Jungle vines shall come in behind the rifles
and all so quickly, so very, very quickly.
Ay, Wall Street!

The mask. Look at the mask!
And how it spits its forest poison
through New York's imperfect anguish!

December 1929

Paisaje de la multitud que vomita
(Anochecer de Coney Island)

La mujer gorda venía delante
arrancando las raíces y mojando el pergamino de los
    tambores.
La mujer gorda,
que vuelve del revés los pulpos agonizantes.
La mujer gorda, enemiga de la luna,
corría por las calles y los pisos deshabitados
y dejaba por los rincones pequeñas calaveras de paloma
y levantaba las furias de los banquetes de los siglos
    últimos
y llamaba al demonio del pan por las colinas del cielo
    barrido
y filtraba un ansia de luz en las circulaciones
    subterráneas.
Son los cementerios. Lo sé. Son los cementerios
y el dolor de las cocinas enterradas bajo la arena.
Son los muertos, los faisanes y las manzanas de otra
    hora
los que nos empujan en la garganta.

Llegaban los rumores de la selva del vómito
con las mujeres vacías, con niños de cera caliente,
con árboles fermentados y camareros incansables
que sirven platos de sal bajo las arpas de la saliva.
Sin remedio, hijo mío, ¡vomita! No hay remedio.
No es el vómito de los húsares sobre los pechos de la
    prostituta,
ni el vómito del gato que se tragó una rana por
    descuido.

Landscape of a Vomiting Multitude
(Dusk at Coney Island)

The fat lady came first,
tearing out roots and moistening drumskins.
The fat lady
who turns dying octopuses inside out.
The fat lady, the moon's antagonist,
was running through the streets and deserted buildings
and leaving tiny skulls of pigeons in the corners
and stirring up the furies of the last centuries' feasts
and summoning the demon of bread through the sky's
    clean-swept hills
and filtering a longing for light into subterranean
    tunnels.
The graveyards, yes, the graveyards
and the sorrow of the kitchens buried in sand,
the dead, pheasants and apples of another era,
pushing into our throat.

There were murmurings from the jungle of vomit
with the empty women, with hot wax children,
with fermented trees and tireless waiters
who serve platters of salt beneath harps of saliva.
There's no other way, my son, vomit! There's no other
    way.
It's not the vomit of hussars on the breasts of their
    whores,
nor the vomit of cats that inadvertently swallowed
    frogs,

Son los muertos que arañan con sus manos de tierra
las puertas de pedernal donde se pudren nublos y postres.

La mujer gorda venía delante
con las gentes de los barcos y de las tabernas y de los
   jardines.
El vómito agitaba delicadamente sus tambores
entre algunas niñas de sangre
que pedían protección a la luna.
¡Ay de mí! ¡Ay de mí! ¡Ay de mí!
Esta mirada mía fue mía, pero ya no es mía,
esta mirada que tiembla desnuda por el alcohol
y despide barcos increíbles
por las anémonas de los muelles.
Me defiendo con esta mirada
que mana de las ondas por donde el alba no se atreve,
yo, poeta sin brazos, perdido
entre la multitud que vomita,
sin caballo efusivo que corte
los espesos musgos de mis sienes.

Pero la mujer gorda seguía delante
y la gente buscaba las farmacias
donde el amargo trópico se fija.
Sólo cuando izaron la bandera y llegaron los primeros
   canes
la ciudad entera se agolpó en las barandillas del
   embarcadero.

Nueva York, 29 de diciembre 1929

but the dead who scratch with clay hands
on flint gates where clouds and desserts decay.

The fat lady came first
with the crowds from the ships, taverns, and parks.
Vomit was delicately shaking its drums
among a few little girls of blood
who were begging the moon for protection.
Who could imagine my sadness?
The look on my face was mine, but now isn't me,
the naked look on my face, trembling for alcohol
and launching incredible ships
through the anemones of the piers.
I protect myself with this look
that flows from waves where no dawn would go,
I, poet without arms, lost
in the vomiting multitude,
with no effusive horse to shear
the thick moss from my temples.

But the fat lady went first
and the crowds kept looking for the pharmacies
where the bitter tropics could be found.
Only when a flag went up and the first dogs arrived
did the entire city rush to the railings of the boardwalk.

New York, December 29, 1929

Paisaje de la multitud que orina
(Nocturno de Battery Place)

Se quedaron solos:
aguardaban la velocidad de las últimas bicicletas.
Se quedaron solas:
esperaban la muerte de un niño en el velero japonés.
Se quedaron solos y solas,
soñando con los picos abiertos de los pájaros
    agonizantes,
con el agudo quitasol que pincha
al sapo recién aplastado,
bajo un silencio con mil orejas
y diminutas bocas de agua
en los desfiladeros que resisten
el ataque violento de la luna.
Lloraba el niño del velero y se quebraban los corazones
angustiados por el testigo y la vigilia de todas las cosas
y porque todavía en el suelo celeste de negras huellas
gritaban nombres oscuros, salivas y radios de níquel.
No importa que el niño calle cuando le claven el último
    alfiler,
ni importa la derrota de la brisa en la corola del algodón,
porque hay un mundo de la muerte con marineros
    definitivos
que se asomarán a los arcos y os helarán por detrás de
    los árboles.
Es inútil buscar el recodo
donde la noche olvida su viaje
y acechar un silencio que no tenga
trajes rotos y cáscaras y llanto,
porque tan sólo el diminuto banquete de la araña

Landscape of a Pissing Multitude
(Battery Place Nocturne)

The men kept to themselves:
they were waiting for the swiftness of the last cyclists.
The women kept to themselves:
they were expecting the death of a boy on a Japanese
   schooner.
They all kept to themselves—
dreaming of the open beaks of dying birds,
the sharp parasol that punctures
a recently flattened toad,
beneath silence with a thousand ears
and tiny mouths of water
in the canyons that resist
the violent attack of the moon.
The boy on the schooner was crying and hearts were
   breaking
in anguish for the witness and the vigilance of all things,
and because on the sky-blue ground of black footprints,
obscure names, saliva, and chrome radios were still
   crying.
It doesn't matter if the boy grows silent when stuck
   with the last pin,
or if the breeze is defeated in cupped cotton flowers,
because there is a world of death whose perpetual sailors
will appear in the arches and freeze you from behind the
   trees.
It's useless to look for the bend
where night loses its way
and to wait in ambush for a silence that has no
torn clothes, no shells, and no tears,
because even the tiny banquet of a spider

57.

basta para romper el equilibrio de todo el cielo.
No hay remedio para el gemido del velero japonés,
ni para estas gentes ocultas que tropiezan con las
esquinas.
El campo se muerde la cola para unir las raíces en un
punto
y el ovillo busca por la grama su ansia de longitud
insatisfecha.
¡La luna! Los policías. ¡Las sirenas de los transatlánticos!
Fachadas de orín, de humo, anémonas, guantes de
goma.
Todo está roto por la noche,
abierta de piernas sobre las terrazas.
Todo está roto por los tibios caños
de una terrible fuente silenciosa.
¡Oh gentes! ¡Oh mujercillas! ¡Oh soldados!
Será preciso viajar por los ojos de los idiotas,
campos libres donde silban las mansas cobras de
alambradas,
paisajes llenos de sepulcros que producen fresquísimas
manzanas,
para que venga la luz desmedida
que temen los ricos detrás de sus lupas,
el olor de un solo cuerpo con la doble vertiente de lis y
rata
y para que se quemen estas gentes que pueden orinar
alrededor de un gemido
o en los cristales donde se comprenden las olas nunca
repetidas.

is enough to upset the entire equilibrium of the sky.
There is no cure for the moaning from a Japanese
    schooner,
nor for those shadowy people who stumble on the
    curbs.
The countryside bites its own tail in order to gather a
    bunch of roots
and a ball of yarn looks anxiously in the grass for
    unrealized longitude.
The moon! The police. The foghorns of the ocean liners!
Façades of urine, of smoke, anemones, rubber gloves.
Everything is shattered in the night
that spreads its legs on the terraces.
Everything is shattered in the tepid faucets
of a terrible silent fountain.
Oh, crowds! Loose women! Soldiers!
We will have to journey through the eyes of idiots,
open country where the docile cobras, coiled like wire,
    hiss,
landscapes full of graves that yield the freshest apples,
so that uncontrollable light will arrive
to frighten the rich behind their magnifying glasses—
the odor of a single corpse from the double source of
    lily and rat—
and so that fire will consume those crowds still able to
    piss around a moan
or on the crystals in which each inimitable wave is
    understood.

Asesinato
(Dos voces de madrugada en Riverside Drive)

—*¿Cómo fue?*
—Una grieta en la mejilla.
¡Eso es todo!
Una uña que aprieta el tallo.
Un alfiler que bucea
hasta encontrar las raicillas del grito.
Y el mar deja de moverse.
—*¿Cómo, cómo fue?*
—Así.
—*¡Déjame! ¿De esa manera?*
—Sí.
El corazón salió solo.
—*¡Ay, ay de mí!*

Murder
(Two Early Morning Voices on Riverside Drive)

"How did it happen?"
"A gash on the cheek.
That's all!
A fingernail that pinches the stem.
A pin that dives
until it finds the roots of a scream.
And the sea stops still."
"How, how did it happen?"
"Like this."
"Really! Like that?"
"Yes.
The heart came out on its own."
"I'm done for!"

Navidad en el Hudson

¡Esa esponja gris!
Ese marinero recién degollado.
Ese río grande.
Esa brisa de límites oscuros.
Ese filo, amor, ese filo.
Estaban los cuatro marineros luchando con el mundo.
Con el mundo de aristas que ven todos los ojos.
Con el mundo que no se puede recorrer sin caballos.
Estaban uno, cien, mil marineros
luchando con el mundo de las agudas velocidades,
sin enterarse de que el mundo
estaba solo por el cielo.

El mundo solo por el cielo solo.
Son las colinas de martillos y el triunfo de la hierba
    espesa.
Son los vivísimos hormigueros y las monedas en el
    fango.
El mundo solo por el cielo solo
y el aire a la salida de todas las aldeas.

Cantaba la lombriz el terror de la rueda
y el marinero degollado
cantaba al oso de agua que lo había de estrechar;
y todos cantaban aleluya,
aleluya. Cielo desierto.
Es lo mismo, ¡lo mismo!, aleluya.

He pasado toda la noche en los andamios de los arrabales
dejándome la sangre por la escayola de los proyectos,
ayudando a los marineros a recoger las velas
    desgarradas.

62.

Christmas on the Hudson

That gray sponge!
That sailor whose throat was just cut.
That great river.
Those dark boundaries of the breeze.
That keen blade, my love, that keen blade.
The four sailors wrestled with the world.
With that sharp-edged world that all eyes see.
With the world we couldn't traverse without horses.
One, a hundred, a thousand sailors
wrestling with the world of keen-edged velocities,
unaware that the world
was alone in the sky.

The world alone in the lonely sky.
Hills of hammers and the thick grass's triumph.
Teeming anthills and coins in the mire.
The world alone in the lonely sky,
and the air where all the villages end.

The earthworm sang its terror of the wheel,
and the sailor whose throat was slashed
sang to the water-bear that held him close;
and they were all singing alleluia,
alleluia. Deserted sky.
It's all the same—the same!—alleluia.

I stood all night on scaffolding in the boroughs,
leaving my blood on the stucco projects,
helping the sailors lower their ripped sails.

Y estoy con las manos vacías en el rumor de la
    desembocadura.
No importa que cada minuto
un niño nuevo agite sus ramitos de venas,
ni que el parto de la víbora, desatado bajo las ramas,
calme la sed de sangre de los que miran el desnudo.
Lo que importa es esto: hueco. Mundo solo.
    Desembocadura.
Alba no. Fábula inerte.
Sólo esto: desembocadura.
¡Oh esponja mía gris!
¡Oh cuello mío recién degollado!
¡Oh río grande mío!
¡Oh brisa mía de límites que no son míos!
¡Oh filo de mi amor, oh hiriente filo!

Nueva York, 27 de diciembre 1929

And I stand with empty hands in the murmur of the
  river's mouth.
It doesn't matter if every minute
a newborn child waves the little branches of its veins,
or if a newborn viper, uncoiling beneath the branches,
calms the blood lust of those who watch the naked man.
What matters is this: emptied space. Lonely world.
  River's mouth.
Not dawn. Idle fable.
This alone: river's mouth.
Oh, my gray sponge!
Oh, my throat just cut open!
Oh, my great river!
Oh, my breeze's boundaries that are not mine!
Oh, the keen blade of my love, oh, the cutting blade!

New York, December 27, 1929

Ciudad sin sueño
(Nocturno del Brooklyn Bridge)

No duerme nadie por el cielo. Nadie, nadie.
No duerme nadie.
Las criaturas de la luna huelen y rondan las cabañas.
Vendrán las iguanas vivas a morder a los hombres que
   no sueñan
y el que huye con el corazón roto encontrará por las
   esquinas
al increíble cocodrilo quieto bajo la tierna protesta de los
   astros.

No duerme nadie por el mundo. Nadie, nadie.
No duerme nadie.
Hay un muerto en el cementerio más lejano
que se queja tres años
porque tiene un paisaje seco en la rodilla;
y el niño que enterraron esta mañana lloraba tanto
que hubo necesidad de llamar a los perros para que
   callase.

No es sueño la vida. ¡Alerta! ¡Alerta! ¡Alerta!
Nos caemos por las escaleras para comer la tierra
   húmeda
o subimos al filo de la nieve con el coro de las dalias
   muertas.
Pero no hay olvido ni sueño:
carne viva. Los besos atan las bocas
en una maraña de venas recientes
y al que le duele su dolor le dolerá sin descanso
y el que teme la muerte la llevará sobre los hombros.

Sleepless City
(Brooklyn Bridge Nocturne)

Out in the sky, no one sleeps. No one, no one.
No one sleeps.
Lunar creatures sniff and circle the dwellings.
Live iguanas will come to bite the men who don't
  dream,
and the brokenhearted fugitive will meet on street
  corners
an incredible crocodile resting beneath the tender protest
  of the stars.

Out in the world, no one sleeps. No one, no one.
No one sleeps.
There is a corpse in the farthest graveyard
complaining for three years
because of an arid landscape in his knee;
and a boy who was buried this morning cried so much
they had to call the dogs to quiet him.

Life is no dream. Watch out! Watch out! Watch out!
We fall down stairs and eat the moist earth,
or we climb to the snow's edge with the choir of dead
  dahlias.
But there is no oblivion, no dream:
raw flesh. Kisses tie mouths
in a tangle of new veins
and those who are hurt will hurt without rest
and those who are frightened by death will carry it on
  their shoulders.

Un día
los caballos vivirán en las tabernas
y las hormigas furiosas
atacarán los cielos amarillos que se refugian en los ojos
    de las vacas.
Otro día
veremos la resurrección de las mariposas disecadas
y aun andando por un paisaje de esponjas grises y barcos
    mudos
veremos brillar nuestro anillo y manar rosas de nuestra
    lengua.

¡Alerta! ¡Alerta! ¡Alerta!
A los que guardan todavía huellas de zarpa y aguacero,
a aquel muchacho que llora porque no sabe la invención
    del puente
o a aquel muerto que ya no tiene más que la cabeza y un
    zapato,
hay que llevarlos al muro donde iguanas y sierpes
    esperan,
donde espera la dentadura del oso,
donde espera la mano momificada del niño
y la piel del camello se eriza con un violento escalofrío
    azul.

No duerme nadie por el cielo. Nadie, nadie.
No duerme nadie.
Pero si alguien cierra los ojos,
¡azotadlo, hijos míos, azotadlo!
Haya un panorama de ojos abiertos
y amargas llagas encendidas.
No duerme nadie por el mundo. Nadie, nadie.
Ya lo he dicho.
No duerme nadie.

One day
horses will live in the taverns
and furious ants
will attack the yellow skies that take refuge in the eyes
    of cattle.
Another day
we'll witness the resurrection of dried butterflies,
and still walking in a landscape of gray sponges and
    silent ships,
we'll see our ring shine and roses spill from our
    tongues.

Watch out! Watch out! Watch out!
Those still marked by claws and cloudburst,
that boy who cries because he doesn't know about the
    invention of bridges,
or that corpse that has nothing more than its head and
    one shoe—
they all must be led to the wall where iguanas and
    serpents wait,
where the bear's teeth wait,
where the mummified hand of a child waits
and the camel's fur bristles with a violent blue chill.

Out in the sky, no one sleeps. No one, no one.
No one sleeps.
But if someone closes his eyes,
whip him, my children, whip him!
Let there be a panorama of open eyes
and bitter inflamed wounds.
Out in the world, no one sleeps. No one. No one.
I've said it before.
No one sleeps.

Pero si alguien tiene por la noche exceso de musgo en
   las sienes,
abrid los escotillones para que vea bajo la luna
las copas falsas, el veneno y la calavera de los teatros.

much moss on his

see in moonlight
nd the skull of the

Panorama ciego de Nueva York

Si no son los pájaros
cubiertos de ceniza,
si no son los gemidos que golpean las ventanas de la
    boda,
serán las delicadas criaturas del aire
que manan la sangre nueva por la oscuridad
    inextinguible.
Pero no, no son los pájaros,
porque los pájaros están a punto de ser bueyes.
Pueden ser rocas blancas con la ayuda de la luna
y son siempre muchachas heridas
antes de que los jueces levanten la tela.

Todos comprenden el dolor que se relaciona con la
    muerte,
pero el verdadero dolor no está presente en el espíritu.
No está en el aire, ni en nuestra vida,
ni en estas terrazas llenas de humo.
El verdadero dolor que mantiene despiertas las cosas
es una pequeña quemadura infinita
en los ojos inocentes de los otros sistemas.

Un traje abandonado pesa tanto en los hombros
que muchas veces el cielo los agrupa en ásperas manadas;
y las que mueren de parto saben en la última hora
que todo rumor será piedra y toda huella latido.
Nosotros ignoramos que el pensamiento tiene arrabales
donde el filósofo es devorado por los chinos y las orugas
y algunos niños idiotas han encontrado por las cocinas
pequeñas golondrinas con muletas
que sabían pronunciar la palabra amor.

Blind Panorama of New York

If it isn't the birds
covered with ash,
if it isn't the cries beating against the windows of the
    wedding,
it is the delicate creatures of the air
that spill fresh blood in the inextinguishable darkness.
But no, it isn't the birds,
because the birds will soon become oxen.
They could become white rocks with the moon's help
and they are always wounded girls
before the judges lift the cloth.

Everyone understands the pain that accompanies death,
but genuine pain doesn't live in the spirit,
nor in the air, nor in our lives,
nor on these terraces of billowing smoke.
The genuine pain that keeps everything awake
is a tiny, infinite burn
on the innocent eyes of other systems.

An abandoned suit weighs so heavily on the shoulders
that the sky often shrugs them into ragged togetherness.
And those who die in childbirth learn in their last hour
that every murmur will be stone and every footstep will
    throb.
We forget that the mind has boroughs
where Chinese and caterpillars devour the philosopher.
And some feebleminded children in the kitchens have
    discovered
tiny swallows on crutches
that could pronounce the word love.

No, no son los pájaros.
No es un pájaro el que expresa la turbia fiebre de
    laguna,
ni el ansia de asesinato que nos oprime cada momento,
ni el metálico rumor de suicidio que nos anima cada
    madrugada:
es una cápsula de aire donde nos duele todo el mundo,
es un pequeño espacio vivo al loco unisón de la luz,
es una escala indefinible donde las nubes y rosas olvidan
el griterío chino que bulle por el desembarcadero de la
    sangre.
Yo muchas veces me he perdido
para buscar la quemadura que mantiene despiertas las
    cosas
y sólo he encontrado marineros echados sobre las
    barandillas
y pequeñas criaturas del cielo enterradas bajo la nieve.
Pero el verdadero dolor estaba en otras plazas
donde los peces cristalizados agonizaban dentro de los
    troncos;
plazas del cielo extraño para las antiguas estatuas ilesas
y para la tierna intimidad de los volcanes.

No hay dolor en la voz. Sólo existen los dientes,
pero dientes que callarán aislados por el raso negro.
No hay dolor en la voz. Aquí sólo existe la Tierra.
La Tierra con sus puertas de siempre
que llevan al rubor de los frutos.

No, it isn't the birds.
A bird can't express the troubled fever of a lagoon
or the urge to murder someone that oppresses us every
    moment,
or the metallic hum of suicide that revives us every
    morning.
It's a capsule of air where we suffer the whole world,
a tiny space alive in the crazy unison of light,
an indefinable ladder on which clouds and roses forget
the Chinese howl that boils over on the waterfront of
    the blood.
I've often lost myself
in order to find the burn that keeps everything awake
and all I've found are sailors leaning over the railings
and tiny sky creatures buried under the snow.
But genuine pain was on other plazas
where crystallized fish were dying inside tree trunks;
plazas of blue sky alien to the unscathed statues of
    antiquity
and to the intimate tenderness of volcanoes.

There is no pain in the voice. Only the teeth exist,
but isolated teeth that will be silenced by black satin.
There is no pain in the voice. Only the Earth exists
    here.
The Earth and its timeless doors
which lead to the blush of the fruit.

Nacimiento de Cristo

Un pastor pide teta por la nieve que ondula
blancos perros tendidos entre linternas sordas.
El Cristito de barro se ha partido los dedos
en los filos eternos de la madera rota.

¡Ya vienen las hormigas y los pies ateridos!
Dos hilillos de sangre quiebran el cielo duro.
Los vientres del demonio resuenan por los valles
golpes y resonancias de carne de molusco.

Lobos y sapos cantan en las hogueras verdes
coronadas por vivos hormigueros del alba.
La mula tiene un sueño de grandes abanicos
y el toro sueña un toro de agujeros y de agua.

El niño llora y mira con un tres en la frente.
San José ve en el heno tres espinas de bronce.
Los pañales exhalan un rumor de desierto
con cítaras sin cuerdas y degolladas voces.

La nieve de Manhattan empuja los anuncios
y lleva gracia pura por las falsas ojivas.
Sacerdotes idiotas y querubes de pluma
van detrás de Lutero por las altas esquinas.

The Birth of Christ

A shepherd begs to be suckled in snow that drifts
white dogs stretched out between shaded lanterns.
The little clay Christ has split its fingers
on the eternally keen edges of the splintered wood.

Here come the ants and the feet stiff with cold!
Two small threads of blood break up the hard sky.
The demon's intestines growl through the stricken
valleys and the resonant flesh of mollusks.

Wolves and toads sing in green bonfires
crowned by the flaming anthills of dawn.
The mule has a dream of enormous fans
and the bull dreams a pierced bull and water.

The child with a three on its forehead cries and stares.
St. Joseph sees three bronze thorns in the hay.
And the swaddling clothes exhale the desert's rumbling
with stringless zithers and beheaded voices.

The snow of Manhattan blows against billboards
and carries pure grace through the fake Gothic arches.
Idiot clergymen and cherubim in feathers
follow Luther in a line around the high corners.

IV

POEMAS DEL

LAGO EDEN

MILLS

A Eduardo Ugarte

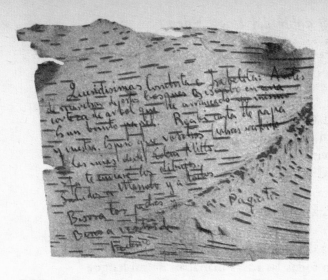

IV

POEMS OF

LAKE EDEN

MILLS

To Eduardo Ugarte

["Autumn in New England." Lorca's letter
to his sisters, Conchita and Isabel, written
from Lake Eden Mills, Vermont, on a piece
of birch bark, August 1929]

Poema doble del Lago Eden

Nuestro ganado pace, el viento espira.

—GARCILASO

Era mi voz antigua
ignorante de los densos jugos amargos.
La adivino lamiendo mis pies
bajo los frágiles helechos mojados.

¡Ay, voz antigua de mi amor,
ay, voz de mi verdad,
ay, voz de mi abierto costado,
cuando todas las rosas manaban de mi lengua
y el césped no conocía la impasible dentadura del
    caballo!

Estás aquí bebiendo mi sangre,
bebiendo mi humor de niño pasado,
mientras mis ojos se quiebran en el viento
con el aluminio y las voces de los borrachos.

Dejarme pasar la puerta
donde Eva come hormigas
y Adán fecunda peces deslumbrados.
Dejarme pasar, hombrecillos de los cuernos,
al bosque de los desperezos
y los alegrísimos saltos.

Yo sé el uso más secreto
que tiene un viejo alfiler oxidado
y sé del horror de unos ojos despiertos
sobre la superficie concreta del plato.

80.

Double Poem of Lake Eden

Our cattle graze, the wind sends forth its breath.
—GARCILASO

It was my ancient voice,
ignorant of the dense and bitter sap.
I foresee it lapping at my feet
beneath the moist and fragile ferns.

Ay, my love's ancient voice,
ay, voice of my truth,
ay, voice of my open side,
when all the roses spilled from my tongue
and the grass hadn't felt the horse's impassable teeth!

Here you are drinking my blood,
drinking the humor of the child I was,
while my eyes are battered by aluminum
and drunken voices in the wind.

Let me pass through the arch
where Eve devours ants
and Adam impregnates the dazzling fish.
Little men with horns, let me return
to the grove of leisure
and the somersaults of pure joy.

I know a ceremony so secret
it requires an old rusty pin,
and I know the horror of open eyes
on the concrete surface of a plate.

81.

Pero no quiero mundo ni sueño, voz divina,
quiero mi libertad, mi amor humano
en el rincón más oscuro de la brisa que nadie quiera.
¡Mi amor humano!

Esos perros marinos se persiguen
y el viento acecha troncos descuidados.
¡Oh voz antigua, quema con tu lengua
esta voz de hojalata y de talco!

Quiero llorar porque me da la gana,
como lloran los niños del último banco,
porque yo no soy un hombre, ni un poeta, ni una hoja,
pero sí un pulso herido que ronda las cosas del otro
    lado.

Quiero llorar diciendo mi nombre,
rosa, niño y abeto a la orilla de este lago,
para decir mi verdad de hombre de sangre
matando en mí la burla y la sugestión del vocablo.

No, no. Yo no pregunto, yo deseo,
voz mía libertada que me lames las manos.
En el laberinto de biombos es mi desnudo el que recibe
la luna de castigo y el reloj encenizado.

Así hablaba yo.
Así hablaba yo cuando Saturno detuvo los trenes
y la bruma y el Sueño y la Muerte me estaban buscando.
Me estaban buscando
allí donde mugen las vacas que tienen patitas de paje
y allí donde flota mi cuerpo entre los equilibrios
    contrarios.

82.

But I want neither world nor dream, divine voice,
I want my liberty, my human love
in the darkest corner of the breeze no one wants.
My human love!

Those sea-dogs chase each other
and the wind lies in ambush for careless tree trunks.
Oh, ancient voice, let your tongue burn
this voice of tin and talc!

I want to cry because I feel like it—
the way children cry in the last row of seats—
because I'm not a man, not a poet, not a leaf,
only a wounded pulse that circles the things of the other
    side.

I want to cry saying my name,
rose, child, and fir on the shore of this lake,
to speak truly as a man of blood
killing in myself the mockery and the suggestive power
    of the word.

No, no, I'm not asking, I'm telling you what I want,
my liberated voice lapping at my hands.
In the labyrinth of folding screens it is my naked body
    that receives
the punishing moon and the clock covered with ash.

I was speaking that way.
I was speaking that way when Saturn stopped the trains
and the fog and the Dream and Death were looking for
    me.
Looking for me
where cattle with the little feet of a page bellow
and my body floats between contrary equilibriums.

83.

Cielo vivo

Yo no podré quejarme
si no encontré lo que buscaba.
Cerca de las piedras sin jugo y los insectos vacíos
no veré el duelo del sol con las criaturas en carne viva.

Pero me iré al primer paisaje
de choques, líquidos y rumores
que trasmina a niño recién nacido
y donde toda superficie es evitada,
para entender que lo que busco tendrá su blanco de
   alegría
cuando yo vuele mezclado con el amor y las arenas.

Allí no llega la escarcha de los ojos apagados
ni el mugido del árbol asesinado por la oruga.
Allí todas las formas guardan entrelazadas
una sola expresión frenética de avance.

No puedes avanzar por los enjambres de corolas
porque el aire disuelve tus dientes de azúcar,
ni puedes acariciar la fugaz hoja del helecho
sin sentir el asombro definitivo del marfil.

Allí bajo las raíces y en la médula del aire,
se comprende la verdad de las cosas equivocadas.
El nadador de níquel que acecha la onda más fina
y el rebaño de vacas nocturnas con rojas patitas de
   mujer.

Living Sky

I won't be able to complain
though I never found what I was looking for.
Near the dried-up stones and the husks of insects,
I won't see the sun's duel with the creatures of flesh and
    blood.

But I'll go to the first landscape
of shocks, fluids, and murmurs
that seeps into a newborn child,
and where all surfaces are avoided,
so I'll know that my search has a joyful target
when I'm flying, jumbled with love and sandstorms.

There, the frost of burned-out eyes won't reach,
nor the bellowing of a tree, murdered by the caterpillar.
There, all the shapes intertwine and have
the same frenetic, forward expression.

You can't pass through the swarming corollas—
the air dissolves your teeth of sugar.
And you can't caress the elusive fern
without feeling the utter astonishment of ivory.

There, under roots and in the medulla of the air,
erroneous things are understood as true.
The chrome swimmer who secretly awaits the finest
    wave
and the flock of nocturnal cattle with a woman's little
    red feet . . .

85.

Yo no podré quejarme
si no encontré lo que buscaba,
pero me iré al primer paisaje de humedades y latidos
para entender que lo que busco tendrá su blanco de
   alegría
cuando yo vuele mezclado con el amor y las arenas.

Vuelo fresco de siempre sobre lechos vacíos.
Sobre grupos de brisas y barcos encallados.
Tropiezo vacilante por la dura eternidad fija
y amor al fin sin alba. Amor. ¡Amor visible!

Eden Mills, Vermont, 24 de agosto 1929

I won't be able to complain
though I never found what I was looking for;
but I'll go to the first fluid landscape of heartbeats
so I'll know that my search has a joyful target
when I'm flying, jumbled with love and sandstorms.

I'm used to the cool air when I fly over empty beds.
Over squalls and ships run aground.
I stumble sleepily through eternity's fixed hardness
and love at the end without dawn. Love. Visible love!

Eden Mills, Vermont, August 24, 1929

V

EN LA

CABAÑA

DEL FARMER

(Campo de

Newburgh)

A Concha Méndez
y Manuel Altolaguirre

V

IN THE
FARMER'S
CABIN

(In the Newburgh
Countryside)

*To Concha Méndez
and Manuel Altolaguirre*

[Lorca with Stanton and Helen Hogan,
Shandaken, New York, September 1929]

El niño Stanton

—*Do you like me?*
—*Yes, and you?*
—*Yes, yes.*

Cuando me quedo solo
me quedan todavía tus diez años,
los tres caballos ciegos,
tus quince rostros con el rostro de la pedrada
y las fiebres pequeñas heladas sobre las hojas del maíz.
Stanton, hijo mío, Stanton.
A las doce de la noche el cáncer salía por los pasillos
y hablaba con los caracoles vacíos de los documentos,
el vivísimo cáncer lleno de nubes y termómetros
con su casto afán de manzana para que lo piquen los
   ruiseñores.
En la casa donde hay un cáncer
se quiebran las blancas paredes en el delirio de la
   astronomía
y por los establos más pequeños y en las cruces de los
   bosques
brilla por muchos años el fulgor de la quemadura.
Mi dolor sangraba por las tardes
cuando tus ojos eran dos muros,
cuando tus manos eran dos países
y mi cuerpo rumor de hierba.
Mi agonía buscaba su traje,
polvorienta, mordida por los perros,
y tú la acompañaste sin temblar
hasta la puerta del agua oscura.
¡Oh mi Stanton, idiota y bello entre los pequeños
   animalitos,

Little Stanton

"Do you like me?"
"Yes, and you?"
"Yes, yes."

When I'm by myself
your ten years stay with me.
So do the three blind horses,
your fifteen faces with the face after the stoning
and tiny frozen fevers on leaves of corn.
Stanton, my son, Stanton.
At twelve midnight, cancer wandered through the
    corridors
and spoke with the documents' empty snails,
cancer springing to life, full of clouds and
    thermometers,
with an apple's chaste longing to be pecked by
    nightingales.
In the house where there is cancer,
the white walls shatter in the delirium of astronomy
and the burn glows brightly for many years
in the tiny stables, in forests where paths intersect.
My sorrow bled in the afternoons
when your eyes became two walls,
when your hands became two countries
and my body murmured like grass.
My agony went looking for its clothes,
dusty, bitten by dogs,
and you went with it, without trembling,
to the threshold of dark water.
Oh, Stanton, idiotic and beautiful among the little
    animals,

91.

con tu madre fracturada por los herreros de las aldeas,
con un hermano bajo los arcos,
otro comido por los hormigueros,
y el cáncer sin alambradas latiendo por las habitaciones!
Hay nodrizas que dan a los niños
ríos de musgo y amargura de pie
y algunas negras suben a los pisos para repartir filtro de
    rata.
Porque es verdad que la gente
quiere echar las palomas a las alcantarillas
y yo sé lo que esperan los que por la calle
nos oprimen de pronto las yemas de los dedos.

Tu ignorancia es un monte de leones, Stanton.
El día que el cáncer te dió una paliza
y te escupió en el dormitorio donde murieron los
    huéspedes en la epidemia
y abrió su quebrada rosa de vidrios secos y manos
    blandas
para salpicar de lodo las pupilas de los que navegan,
tú buscaste en la hierba mi agonía,
mi agonía con flores de terror,
mientras que el agrio cáncer mudo que quiere acostarse
    contigo
pulverizaba rojos paisajes por las sábanas de amargura
y ponía sobre los ataúdes
helados arbolitos de ácido bórico.
Stanton, vete al bosque con tus arpas judías,
vete para aprender celestiales palabras
que duermen en los troncos, en nubes, en tortugas,
en los perros dormidos, en el plomo, en el viento,

your mother hammered to pieces by the village
    blacksmiths,
one brother under the arches
and the other one eaten by the anthills,
and cancer, free of wires, beating in the rooms like a
    heart!
There are wet nurses who give children
rivers of moss and bitter feet,
and black women who spread love potions made from
    rats in the bedrooms upstairs.
Because it's true, there are people
who want to dump doves in the sewers
and I know what else they want—the people
hanging out in the street who suddenly squeeze our
    fingertips.

Your ignorance is a mountain of lions, Stanton.
The day cancer gave you a whipping,
and spit on you in the bedroom where the guests died in
    the epidemic,
and opened its broken rose of dry glass and soft hands
to spatter mud in the eyes of sailors—
you looked for my agony in the grass,
the terrible flowers of my agony,
while the speechless, acid cancer that wants to go to bed
    with you
pulverized red landscapes on the bedsheets of bitterness
and placed on the coffins
little frozen trees of boric acid.
Stanton, go to the woods with your jew's-harp,
go to learn celestial words
that sleep in tree trunks, clouds, and turtles,
in sleeping dogs, in lead and wind,

en lirios que no duermen, en aguas que no copian,
para que aprendas, hijo, lo que tu pueblo olvida.

Cuando empiece el tumulto de la guerra
dejaré un pedazo de queso para tu perro en la oficina.
Tus diez años serán las hojas
que vuelan en los trajes de los muertos,
diez rosas de azufre débil
en el hombro de mi madrugada.
Y yo, Stanton, yo solo, en olvido,
con tus caras marchitas sobre mi boca,
iré penetrando a voces las verdes estatuas de la Malaria.

in irises that don't sleep and water that copies nothing.
Go to learn, my son, what your people forget.

When the thunder of war begins,
I'll leave a piece of cheese for your dog in the office.
Your ten years will be the leaves
flying in the clothes of the dead,
ten roses of powerless sulfur
on the shoulder of my dawn.
And I, Stanton, by myself, forgotten,
your withered faces on my mouth—
I'll go shouting my way through the green statues of
    Malaria.

Vaca

A Luis Lacasa

Se tendió la vaca herida.
Árboles y arroyos trepaban por sus cuernos.
Su hocico sangraba en el cielo.

Su hocico de abejas
bajo el bigote lento de la baba.
Un alarido blanco puso en pie la mañana.

Las vacas muertas y las vivas,
rubor de luz o miel de establo,
balaban con los ojos entornados.

Que se enteren las raíces
y aquel niño que afila su navaja
de que ya se pueden comer la vaca.

Arriba palidecen
luces y yugulares.
Cuatro pezuñas tiemblan en el aire.

Que se entere la luna
y esa noche de rocas amarillas
que ya se fue la vaca de ceniza.

Que ya se fue balando
por el derribo de los cielos yertos,
donde meriendan muerte los borrachos.

Cow

To Luis Lacasa

The wounded cow lay down,
trees and streams climbing over its horns.
Its muzzle bled in the sky.

Its muzzle of bees
under the slow mustache of slobber.
A white cry brought the morning to its feet.

Cows, dead and alive,
blushing light or honey from the stables,
bellowed with half-closed eyes.

Tell the roots
and that child sharpening his knife:
now they can eat the cow.

Above them, lights
and jugulars turn pale.
Four cloven hoofs tremble in the air.

Tell the moon
and that night of yellow rocks:
now the cow of ash has gone.

Now it has gone bellowing
through the wreckage of the rigid skies
where the drunks lunch on death.

Niña ahogada en el pozo
(Granada y Newburgh)

Las estatuas sufren con los ojos por la oscuridad de los
    ataúdes,
pero sufren mucho más por el agua que no
    desemboca . . . ,
que no desemboca.

El pueblo corría por las almenas rompiendo las cañas de
    los pescadores.
¡Pronto! ¡Los bordes! ¡De prisa! Y croaban las estrellas
    tiernas.
. . . que no desemboca.

Tranquila en mi recuerdo, astro, círculo, meta,
lloras por las orillas de un ojo de caballo.
. . . que no desemboca.

Pero nadie en lo oscuro podrá darte distancias,
sino afilado límite: porvenir de diamante.
. . . que no desemboca.

Mientras la gente busca silencios de almohada,
tú lates para siempre definida en tu anillo.
. . . que no desemboca.

Eterna en los finales de unas ondas que aceptan
combate de raíces y soledad prevista.
. . . que no desemboca.

Little Girl Drowned in the Well
(Granada and Newburgh)

Statues suffer the darkness of coffins with their eyes,
but they suffer even more from water that never reaches
   the sea . . .
that never reaches the sea.

The townspeople ran along the battlements, breaking
   the fishermen's poles.
Quickly! To the edge! Hurry! And the tender stars
   sounded like bullfrogs.
. . . that never reaches the sea.

At peace in my memory, heavenly body, circumference,
   boundary,
you cry on the shores of a horse's eye.
. . . that never reaches the sea.

But no one in the darkness will be able to give you
   distances,
only sharpened limits: diamond's future.
. . . that never reaches the sea.

While the people look for pillowed silences,
you pulsate forever, defined by your ring.
. . . that never reaches the sea.

You will always be ahead of some waves that accept
the combat of roots and anticipated solitude.
. . . that never reaches the sea.

¡Ya vienen por las rampas! ¡Levántate del agua!
¡Cada punto de luz te dará una cadena!
. . . que no desemboca.

Pero el pozo te alarga manecitas de musgo,
insospechada ondina de su casta ignorancia.
. . . que no desemboca.

No, que no desemboca. Agua fija en un punto,
respirando con todos sus violines sin cuerdas
en la escala de las heridas y los edificios deshabitados.
¡Agua que no desemboca!

They're coming up the ramps! Arise from the water!
Every point of light will toss you a chain!
. . . that never reaches the sea.

But the well pulls you back with small mossy hands,
you, unforeseen nymph of its chaste ignorance.
. . . that never reaches the sea.

No, that never reaches the sea. Water fixed in one place,
breathing with all its unstrung violins
on the musical scale of wounds and deserted buildings.
Water that never reaches the sea!

VI

INTRODUCCIÓN

A LA MUERTE

(Poemas de la soledad

en Vermont)

Para Rafael Sánchez Ventura

VI

INTRODUCTION

TO DEATH

(Poems of Solitude

in Vermont)

For Rafael Sánchez Ventura

[García Lorca, *Dead Man*, 1932]

Muerte

A Isidoro de Blas

¡Qué esfuerzo!
¡Qué esfuerzo del caballo
por ser perro!
¡Qué esfuerzo del perro por ser golondrina!
¡Qué esfuerzo de la golondrina por ser abeja!
¡Qué esfuerzo de la abeja por ser caballo!
Y el caballo,
¡qué flecha aguda exprime de la rosa!,
¡qué rosa gris levanta de su belfo!
Y la rosa,
¡qué rebaño de luces y alaridos
ata en el vivo azúcar de su tronco!
Y el azúcar,
¡qué puñalitos sueña en su vigilia!
Y los puñales diminutos,
¡qué luna sin establos, qué desnudos,
piel eterna y rubor, andan buscando!
Y yo, por los aleros,
¡qué serafín de llamas busco y soy!
Pero el arco de yeso,
¡qué grande, qué invisible, qué diminuto,
sin esfuerzo!

Death

To Isidoro de Blas

How hard they try!
How hard the horse tries
to become a dog!
How hard the dog tries to become a swallow!
How hard the swallow tries to become a bee!
How hard the bee tries to become a horse!
And the horse,
what a sharp arrow it yanks from the rose,
what a pale rose rising from its lips!
And the rose,
what a flock of lights and cries
knotted in the living sugar of its trunk!
And the sugar,
what daggers it dreams in its vigils!
And the daggers,
what a moon without stables, what nakedness,
eternal and blushing flesh they seek out!
And I, on the roof's edge,
what a burning angel I look for and am!
But the plaster arch,
how vast, how invisible, how minute,
without even trying!

105.

Nocturno del hueco

I

Para ver que todo se ha ido,
para ver los huecos y los vestidos,
¡dame tu guante de luna,
tu otro guante de hierba,
amor mío!

Puede el aire arrancar los caracoles
muertos sobre el pulmón del elefante
y soplar los gusanos ateridos
de las yemas de luz o las manzanas.

Los rostros bogan impasibles
bajo el diminuto griterío de las hierbas
y en el rincón está el pechito de la rana,
turbio de corazón y mandolina.

En la gran plaza desierta
mugía la bovina cabeza recién cortada
y eran duro cristal definitivo
las formas que buscaban el giro de la sierpe.

Para ver que todo se ha ido
dame tu mudo hueco, ¡amor mío!
Nostalgia de academia y cielo triste.
¡Para ver que todo se ha ido!

Dentro de ti, amor mío, por tu carne,
¡qué silencio de trenes boca arriba!,

Nocturne of Emptied Space

I

If you want to see that nothing is left,
see the emptied spaces and the clothes,
give me your lunar glove,
your other glove of grass,
my love!

The air can tear dead snails
from the elephant's lung
and blow the stiff, cold worms
from budding light or apples.

Faces erased of all emotion sail
beneath the faint uproar of the grass
and the frog's little breast is in the corner
with a clouded heart and mandolin.

On the great deserted plaza,
the cow's freshly severed head kept bellowing
and shapes that looked for the serpent's coiling
crystallized completely.

If you want to see that nothing is left,
give me your speechless, emptied space, my love,
grade-school nostalgia and sad sky!
If you want to see that nothing is left!

Inside you, my love, in your flesh,
the silence of derailed trains!

107.

¡cuánto brazo de momia florecido!
¡qué cielo sin salida, amor, qué cielo!

Es la piedra en el agua y es la voz en la brisa
bordes de amor que escapan de su tronco sangrante.
Basta tocar el pulso de nuestro amor presente
para que broten flores sobre los otros niños.

Para ver que todo se ha ido.
Para ver los huecos de nubes y ríos.
Dame tus ramos de laurel, amor.
¡Para ver que todo se ha ido!

Ruedan los huecos puros, por mí, por ti, en el alba
conservando las huellas de las ramas de sangre
y algún perfil de yeso tranquilo que dibuja
instantáneo dolor de luna apuntillada.

Mira formas concretas que buscan su vacío.
Perros equivocados y manzanas mordidas.
Mira el ansia, la angustia de un triste mundo fósil
que no encuentra el acento de su primer sollozo.

Cuando busco en la cama los rumores del hilo
has venido, amor mío, a cubrir mi tejado.
El hueco de una hormiga puede llenar el aire,
pero tú vas gimiendo sin norte por mis ojos.

No, por mis ojos no, que ahora me enseñas
cuatro ríos ceñidos en tu brazo.

So many mummies' arms in bloom!
What a dead-end sky, my love, what a sky!

Stone in water, voice on the breeze—
love's limits burst free from their bleeding trunk.
Feeling the pulse of our love today is enough
to make flowers spring from other children.

If you want to see that nothing is left,
see the emptied spaces of clouds and rivers,
give me your laurel hands, my love.
If you want to see that nothing is left!

The pure spaces spin through me, through you, at
    dawn,
preserving the tracks of the bloody branches
and some profile of tranquil plaster that depicts
the punctured moon's instant sorrow.

Look at the concrete shapes in search of their void.
Lost dogs and half-eaten apples.
Look at this sad fossil world, with its anxiety and
    anguish,
a world that can't find the rhythm of its very first sob.

When I search the bed for murmuring thread,
I know you've come, my love, to cover my roof.
The emptied space of an ant can fill the air,
but you moan with nothing to guide you through my
    eyes.

No, not through my eyes, because now you show me
four rivers wrapped tightly around your arm,

109.

En la dura barraca donde la luna prisionera
devora a un marinero delante de los niños.

Para ver que todo se ha ido,
¡amor inexpugnable, amor huido!
No, no me des tu hueco,
¡que ya va por el aire el mío!
¡Ay de ti, ay de mí, de la brisa!
Para ver que todo se ha ido.

II

Yo.
Con el hueco blanquísimo de un caballo,
crines de ceniza. Plaza pura y doblada.

Yo.
Mi hueco traspasado con las axilas rotas.
Piel seca de uva neutra y amianto de madrugada.

Toda la luz del mundo cabe dentro de un ojo.
Canta el gallo y su canto dura más que sus alas.

Yo.
Con el hueco blanquísimo de un caballo.
Rodeado de espectadores que tienen hormigas en las
    palabras.

En el circo del frío sin perfil mutilado.
Por los capiteles rotos de las mejillas desangradas.

110.

in the hard stockade where the imprisoned moon
devours a sailor in front of the children.

If you want to see that nothing is left,
my impenetrable love, now that you have gone,
don't give me your emptied space. No.
Mine is already traveling through the air!
Who will pity you, or me, or the breeze?
If you want to see that nothing is left.

II

Me.
With the white, white space of a horse,
ashen-maned. Pure and folded plaza.

Me.
My emptied space pierced with what remains of my
   armpits.
Like a neutered grape's shriveled skin and asbestos at
   dawn.

All the world's light fits inside an eye.
The rooster crows and his song lasts longer than his wings.

Me.
With the white, white space of a horse.
Ringed by onlookers with their ant-teeming words.

In the circus of cold weather with no mutilated profile.
Among the chipped columns of cheeks bled white.

111.

Yo.
Mi hueco sin ti, ciudad, sin tus muertos que comen.
Ecuestre por mi vida definitivamente anclada.

Yo.

No hay siglo nuevo ni luz reciente.
Sólo un caballo azul y una madrugada.

Me.
My emptied space without you, city, without your
  voracious dead.
Rider through my life finally at anchor.

Me.

No new age. No enlightenment.
Only a blue horse and dawn.

113.

Paisaje con dos tumbas
y un perro asirio

Amigo,
levántate para que oigas aullar
al perro asirio.
Las tres ninfas del cáncer han estado bailando,
hijo mío.
Trajeron unas montañas de lacre rojo
y unas sábanas duras donde estaba el cáncer dormido.
El caballo tenía un ojo en el cuello
y la luna estaba en un cielo tan frío
que tuvo que desgarrarse su monte de Venus
y ahogar en sangre y ceniza los cementerios antiguos.

Amigo,
despierta, que los montes todavía no respiran
y las hierbas de mi corazón están en otro sitio.
No importa que estés lleno de agua de mar.
Yo amé mucho tiempo a un niño
que tenía una plumilla en la lengua
y vivimos cien años dentro de un cuchillo.
Despierta. Calla. Escucha. Incorpórate un poco.
El aullido
es una larga lengua morada que deja
hormigas de espanto y licor de lirios.
Ya viene hacia la roca. ¡No alargues tus raíces!
Se acerca. Gime. No solloces en sueños, amigo.

¡Amigo!
Levántate para que oigas aullar
al perro asirio.

114.

Landscape with Two Graves
and an Assyrian Dog

Friend,
get up and listen
to the Assyrian dog howl.
Cancer's three nymphs have been dancing,
my son.
They carried mountains of red sealing wax
and stiff bed sheets to the place where cancer slept.
The horse had an eye in its neck
and the moon was in a sky so cold
that she had to tear open her mound of Venus
and drown the ancient graveyards in blood and ashes.

Friend,
wake up, the mountains still aren't breathing
and the grass of my heart is somewhere else.
It doesn't matter if you're full of seawater.
For a long time I loved a child
who had a tiny feather on his tongue,
and we lived inside a knife for a hundred years.
Wake up. Be still. Listen. Sit up in your bed.
The howling
is a long purple tongue that releases
terrifying ants and the liquor of irises.
Here it comes toward the rock. Don't spread out your
    roots!
It approaches. Moans. Friend, don't sob in your dreams.

Friend!
Get up and listen
to the Assyrian dog howl.

115.

Ruina

A Regino Sáinz de la Maza

Sin encontrarse.
Viajero por su propio torso blanco.
¡Así iba el aire!

Pronto se vió que la luna
era una calavera de caballo
y el aire una manzana oscura.

Detrás de la ventana,
con látigos y luces, se sentía
la lucha de la arena con el agua.

Yo ví llegar las hierbas
y les eché un cordero que balaba
bajo sus dientecillos y lancetas.

Volaba dentro de una gota
la cáscara de pluma y celuloide
de la primer paloma.

Las nubes en manada
se quedaron dormidas contemplando
el duelo de las rocas con el alba.

Vienen las hierbas, hijo.
Ya suenan sus espadas de saliva
por el cielo vacío.

116.

Ruin

To Regino Sáinz de la Maza

Never finding itself,
traveling through its own white torso,
the air made its way!

Soon it was clear that the moon
was a horse's skull,
and the air, a dark apple.

Behind the window,
with whips and lights, I felt
sand struggling with water.

I saw all the blades of grass arrive
and I threw a bleating lamb
to their little teeth and lancets.

The first dove, encased
in feathers and plastic,
flew inside a single drop.

The herd of clouds
stayed asleep, watching
the duel between rocks and dawn.

Here comes the grass, son.
Its spit-swords ring
through the empty sky.

117.

Mi mano, amor. ¡Las hierbas!
Por los cristales rotos de la casa
la sangre desató sus cabelleras.

Tú sólo y yo quedamos.
Prepara tu esqueleto para el aire.
Yo sólo y tú quedamos.

Prepara tu esqueleto.
Hay que buscar de prisa, amor, de prisa,
nuestro perfil sin sueño.

Hold my hand, my love. The grass!
Through the house's broken windows,
the blood unleashed its waves of hair.

Only you and I are left.
Prepare your skeleton for the air.
We're the only ones who remain.

Prepare your skeleton.
Hurry, love, hurry, we've got to look
for our sleepless profile.

Luna y panorama de los insectos
(Poema de amor)

La luna en el mar riela,
en la lona gime el viento
y alza en blando movimiento
olas de plata y azul.

—E S P R O N C E D A

Mi corazón tendría la forma de un zapato
si cada aldea tuviera una sirena.
Pero la noche es interminable cuando se apoya en los
    enfermos
y hay barcos que buscan ser mirados para poder
    hundirse tranquilos.

Si el aire sopla blandamente
mi corazón tiene la forma de una niña.
Si el aire se niega a salir de los cañaverales
mi corazón tiene la forma de una milenaria boñiga de
    toro.

Bogar, bogar, bogar, bogar,
hacia el batallón de puntas desiguales,
hacia un paisaje de acechos pulverizados.
Noche igual de la nieve, de los sistemas suspendidos.
Y la luna.
¡La luna!
Pero no la luna.
La raposa de las tabernas.
El gallo japonés que se comió los ojos.
Las hierbas masticadas.

120.

Moon and Panorama of the Insects
(Love Poem)

The moon shimmers on the sea,
the wind moans in the sail
and raises gently swelling
blue and silver waves.
—ESPRONCEDA

My heart would take the shape of a shoe
if a siren lived in every village.
But the night never ends when it leans on the sick,
and there are ships that want to be seen in order to sink
   in peace.

If the wind blows softly,
my heart takes the shape of a girl.
If the wind won't leave the cane fields,
my heart takes the shape of a millenary cow pie.

Row, row, row, row,
toward the army of jagged points,
toward a landscape of pulverized ambushes.
Equal night of the snow, the discontinued systems.
And the moon.
The moon!
But not the moon.
The taverns' fox.
The Japanese rooster that ate its own eyes.
The cud.

121.

No nos salvan las solitarias en los vidrios,
ni los herbolarios donde el metafísico
encuentra las otras vertientes del cielo.
Son mentira las formas. Sólo existe
el círculo de bocas del oxígeno.
Y la luna.
Pero no la luna.
Los insectos,
los muertos diminutos por las riberas,
dolor en longitud,
yodo en un punto,
las muchedumbres en el alfiler,
el desnudo que amasa la sangre de todos,
y mi amor que no es un caballo ni una quemadura,
criatura de pecho devorado.
¡Mi amor!

Ya cantan, gritan, gimen: Rostro. ¡Tu rostro! Rostro.
Las manzanas son unas,
las dalias son idénticas,
la luz tiene un sabor de metal acabado
y el campo de todo un lustro cabrá en la mejilla de la
    moneda.
Pero tu rostro cubre los cielos del banquete.
¡Ya cantan!, ¡gritan!, ¡gimen!,
¡cubren!, ¡trepan!, ¡espantan!

Es necesario caminar, ¡de prisa!, por las ondas, por las
    ramas,
por las calles deshabitadas de la Edad Media que bajan al río.

The empty women, alone in store windows, won't
    save us,
nor herbariums where the metaphysician
meets the other slopes of the sky.
Shapes are a lie. What is there?
The circle of mouths of the oxygen.
And the moon.
But not the moon.
The insects,
little dead things lining the shores,
sorrow on longitude,
iodine on stitched flesh,
the crowd on the head of a pin,
the naked man who kneads everyone's blood,
and my love who is neither horse nor burn,
creature whose breast was consumed.
My love!

Now they sing, scream, moan: A face. Your face! A
    face.
The apples are one,
the dahlias identical,
the light tastes like worn-out metal
and the countryside of half a decade will fit on the cheek
    of a coin.
But your face covers the skies of the feast.
Now they sing, scream, moan,
cover everything, climb, terrify!

We've got to move—Hurry up!—through the waves,
    the branches,
the deserted streets of the Middle Ages going down to
    the river,

por las tiendas de las pieles donde suena un cuerno de
   vaca herida,
por las escalas, ¡sin miedo!, por las escalas.
Hay un hombre descolorido que se está bañando en el
   mar;
es tan tierno que los reflectores le comieron jugando el
   corazón.
Y en el Perú viven mil mujeres, ¡oh insectos!, que noche
   y día
hacen nocturnos y desfiles entrecruzando sus propias
   venas.

Un diminuto guante corrosivo me detiene. ¡Basta!
En mi pañuelo he sentido el tris
de la primera vena que se rompe.
Cuida tus pies, amor mío, ¡tus manos!,
ya que yo tengo que entregar mi rostro,
mi rostro, ¡mi rostro!, ¡ay, mi comido rostro!

Este fuego casto para mi deseo,
esta confusión por anhelo de equilibrio,
este inocente dolor de pólvora en mis ojos,
aliviará la angustia de otro corazón
devorado por las nebulosas.

No nos salva la gente de las zapaterías,
ni los paisajes que se hacen música al encontrar las llaves
   oxidadas.
Son mentira los aires. Sólo existe
una cunita en el desván
que recuerda todas las cosas.
Y la luna.
Pero no la luna.
Los insectos.

the stores of hides where a wounded cow's horn
    bellows,
up the ladders—Don't be scared!—up the ladders.
A pallid man is bathing in the sea;
he's so tender that searchlights ate him after gambling
    away his heart.
And a thousand women live in Peru—Oh, insects!—
    night and day
they weave nocturnes and parades among their own
    veins.

One tiny corrosive glove stops me. That's enough!
I feel the crackle of the first
broken vein on my handkerchief.
Watch out for your hands and feet, my love,
since I must give up my face,
my face, my face, yes, my half-eaten face!

This chaste, burning desire of mine,
this confusion from longing for equilibrium,
this innocent sorrow of gunpowder in my eyes,
will lighten the anguish of another heart
consumed by the nebulae.

The people in shoe stores won't save us,
nor the landscapes becoming music when they find the
    rusted keys.
Breezes are a lie. Only a small cradle
exists, in the attic,
that remembers everything.
And the moon.
But not the moon.
The insects.

125.

Los insectos solos,
crepitantes, mordientes, estremecidos, agrupados,
y la luna
con un guante de humo sentada en la puerta de sus
   derribos.
¡¡La luna!!

Nueva York, 4 de enero 1930

Just the insects,
crackling, biting, quivering, swarming,
and the moon
with a smoking glove in the doorway of its wreckage.
The moon!!

New York, January 4, 1930

VII

VUELTA

A LA CIUDAD

Para Antonio Hernández Soriano

VII

RETURN

TO THE CITY

For Antonio Hernández Soriano

[García Lorca, *Self-portrait in New York,*
1929–1932]

Nueva York
(Oficina y denuncia)

A Fernando Vela

Debajo de las multiplicaciones
hay una gota de sangre de pato;
debajo de las divisiones
hay una gota de sangre de marinero;
debajo de las sumas, un río de sangre tierna.
Un río que viene cantando
por los dormitorios de los arrabales,
y es plata, cemento o brisa
en el alba mentida de New York.
Existen las montañas. Lo sé.
Y los anteojos para la sabiduría.
Lo sé. Pero yo no he venido a ver el cielo.
He venido para ver la turbia sangre,
la sangre que lleva las máquinas a las cataratas
y el espíritu a la lengua de la cobra.
Todos los días se matan en New York
cuatro millones de patos,
cinco millones de cerdos,
dos mil palomas para el gusto de los agonizantes,
un millón de vacas,
un millón de corderos
y dos millones de gallos,
que dejan los cielos hechos añicos.

Más vale sollozar afilando la navaja
o asesinar a los perros en las alucinantes cacerías,
que resistir en la madrugada
los interminables trenes de leche,

130.

New York
(Office and Denunciation)

To Fernando Vela

Under the multiplications,
a drop of duck's blood;
under the divisions,
a drop of sailor's blood;
under the additions, a river of tender blood.
A river that sings and flows
past bedrooms in the boroughs—
and it's money, cement, or wind
in New York's counterfeit dawn.
I know the mountains exist.
And wisdom's eyeglasses,
too. But I didn't come to see the sky.
I'm here to see the clouded blood,
the blood that sweeps machines over waterfalls
and the soul toward the cobra's tongue.
Every day in New York, they slaughter
four million ducks,
five million hogs,
two thousand pigeons to accommodate the tastes of the
    dying,
one million cows,
one million lambs,
and two million roosters
that smash the skies to pieces.

It's better to sob while honing the blade
or kill dogs on the delirious hunts
than to resist at dawn
the endless milk trains,

131.

los interminables trenes de sangre
y los trenes de rosas maniatadas
por los comerciantes de perfumes.
Los patos y las palomas,
y los cerdos y los corderos
ponen sus gotas de sangre
debajo de las multiplicaciones,
y los terribles alaridos de las vacas estrujadas
llenan de dolor el valle
donde el Hudson se emborracha con aceite.

Yo denuncio a toda la gente
que ignora la otra mitad,
la mitad irredimible
que levanta sus montes de cemento
donde laten los corazones
de los animalitos que se olvidan
y donde caeremos todos
en la última fiesta de los taladros.
Os escupo en la cara.
La otra mitad me escucha
devorando, orinando, volando en su pureza,
como los niños de las porterías
que llevan frágiles palitos
a los huecos donde se oxidan
las antenas de los insectos.
No es el infierno, es la calle.
No es la muerte. Es la tienda de frutas.
Hay un mundo de ríos quebrados y distancias inasibles
en la patita de ese gato quebrada por un automóvil,
y yo oigo el canto de la lombriz
en el corazón de muchas niñas.
Óxido, fermento, tierra estremecida.

the endless blood trains
and the trains of roses, manacled
by the dealers in perfume.
The ducks and the pigeons,
and the hogs and the lambs
lay their drops of blood
under the multiplications,
and the terrified bellowing of the cows wrung dry
fills the valley with sorrow
where the Hudson gets drunk on oil.

I denounce everyone
who ignores the other half,
the half that can't be redeemed,
who lift their mountains of cement
where the hearts beat
inside forgotten little animals
and where all of us will fall
in the last feast of pneumatic drills.
I spit in all your faces.
The other half hears me,
devouring, pissing, flying in their purity,
like the supers' children in lobbies
who carry fragile twigs
to the emptied spaces where
the insect antennae are rusting.
This is not hell, but the street.
Not death, but the fruit stand.
There is a world of tamed rivers and distances just
    beyond our grasp
in the cat's paw smashed by a car,
and I hear the earthworm's song
in the hearts of many girls.
Rust, fermentation, earth tremor.

133.

Tierra tú mismo que nadas por los números de la
  oficina.
¿Qué voy a hacer, ordenar los paisajes?
¿Ordenar los amores que luego son fotografías,
que luego son pedazos de madera y bocanadas de
  sangre?
No, no; yo denuncio.
Yo denuncio la conjura
de estas desiertas oficinas
que no radian las agonías,
que borran los programas de la selva,
y me ofrezco a ser comido por las vacas estrujadas
cuando sus gritos llenan el valle
donde el Hudson se emborracha con aceite.

You yourself are the earth as you drift in office
    numbers.
What shall I do now? Set the landscapes in order?
Order the loves that soon become photographs,
that soon become pieces of wood and mouthfuls of
    blood?
No, no: I denounce it all.
I denounce the conspiracy
of these deserted offices
that radiate no agony,
that erase the forest's plans,
and I offer myself as food for the cows wrung dry
when their bellowing fills the valley
where the Hudson gets drunk on oil.

135.

Cementerio judío

Las alegres fiebres huyeron a las maromas de los barcos
y el judío empujó la verja con el pudor helado del
  interior de las lechugas.

Los niños de Cristo dormían,
y el agua era una paloma,
y la madera era una garza,
y el plomo era un colibrí,
y aun las vivas prisiones de fuego
estaban consoladas por el salto de la langosta.

Los niños de Cristo bogaban y los judíos llenaban los
  muros
con un solo corazón de paloma
por el que todos querían escapar.
Las niñas de Cristo cantaban y las judías miraban la
  muerte
con un solo ojo de faisán,
vidriado por la angustia de un millón de paisajes.

Los médicos ponen en el níquel sus tijeras y guantes de
  goma
cuando los cadáveres sienten en los pies
la terrible claridad de otra luna enterrada.
Pequeños dolores ilesos se acercan a los hospitales
y los muertos se van quitando un traje de sangre cada
  día.

Las arquitecturas de escarcha,
las liras y gemidos que se escapan de las hojas diminutas
en otoño, mojando las últimas vertientes,
se apagaban en el negro de los sombreros de copa.

136.

Jewish Cemetery

The fevers fled with great joy to the hawsers of moored
    ships
and the Jew chastely pushed against the gate the way
    lettuce grows coldly from its center.

Christ's children slept,
and the water was a dove,
and the wood was a heron,
and the lead was a hummingbird,
and even the living prisons of fire
were consoled by the locust's leap.

Christ's children rowed and the Jews packed the walls
with a single dove's heart
through which all of them wished to escape.
Christ's little girls sang and the Jewish women looked at
    death
with a pheasant's solitary eye,
glazed by the anguish of a million landscapes.

The doctors put their scissors and surgical gloves on the
    chrome table
when the feet of the corpses feel
the terrible brightness of another buried moon.
Tiny unscathed pains approach the hospitals
and the dead take off a suit of blood every day.

The architecture of frost,
the lyres and moans that escape from the small leaves
in autumn, drenching the farthest slopes,
were extinguished in the blackness of their derbies.

137.

La hierba celeste y sola de la que huye con miedo el
    rocío
y las blancas entradas de mármol que conducen al aire
    duro
mostraban su silencio roto por las huellas dormidas de
    los zapatos.

El judío empujó la verja;
pero el judío no era un puerto
y las barcas de nieve se agolparon
por las escalerillas de su corazón:
las barcas de nieve que acechan
un hombre de agua que las ahogue,
las barcas de los cementerios
que a veces dejan ciegos a los visitantes.

Los niños de Cristo dormían
y el judío ocupó su litera.
Tres mil judíos lloraban en el espanto de las galerías
porque reunían entre todos con esfuerzo media paloma,
porque uno tenía la rueda de un reloj
y otro un botín con orugas parlantes
y otro una lluvia nocturna cargada de cadenas
y otro la uña de un ruiseñor que estaba vivo;
y porque la media paloma gemía
derramando una sangre que no era la suya.

Las alegres fiebres bailaban por las cúpulas humedecidas
y la luna copiaba en su mármol
nombres viejos y cintas ajadas.
Llegó la gente que come por detrás de las yertas
    columnas
y los asnos de blancos dientes
con los especialistas de las articulaciones.

138.

The dew retreats in fear from blue, forsaken grass,
and the white marble entrances that lead to hard air
were showing their silence broken by sleeping
   footprints.

The Jew pushed against the gate;
but the Jew was not a port
and the boats of snow piled up
on the gangways of his heart:
the boats that wait in ambush for
a man of water who can drown them,
the boats of the cemeteries
that sometimes blind the visitors.

Christ's children slept
and the Jew lay down in his berth.
Three thousand Jews wept in the galleries of terror
because it was all they could do to gather half a dove
   among themselves,
because one of them had the wheel from a clock
and another a boot laced with talking caterpillars
and another a nocturnal rain burdened with chains
and another the claw of a nightingale that was still alive;
and because the half-dove moaned,
spilling blood that was not its own.

The fevers danced with great joy on the humid domes,
and the moon inscribed in its marble
ancient names and worn ribbons.
Those who dine behind the rigid columns arrived,
so did the donkeys with their white teeth
and the specialists in the body's joints.

139.

Verdes girasoles temblaban
por los páramos del crepúsculo
y todo el cementerio era una queja
de bocas de cartón y trapo seco.
Ya los niños de Cristo se dormían
cuando el judío, apretando los ojos,
se cortó las manos en silencio
al escuchar los primeros gemidos.

Nueva York, 18 de enero 1930

Green sunflowers trembled
on the wastelands of dusk
and the whole cemetery began to complain
with cardboard mouths and dry rags.
Christ's children were going to sleep
when the Jew, squeezing his eyes shut,
silently cut off his hands
as he heard the first moans begin.

New York, January 18, 1930

141.

Crucifixión

La luna pudo detenerse al fin por la curva blanquísima
  de los caballos.
Un rayo de luz violenta que se escapaba de la herida
proyectó en el cielo el instante de la circuncisión de un
  niño muerto.

La sangre bajaba por el monte y los ángeles la buscaban,
pero los cálices eran de viento y al fin llenaba los
  zapatos.
Cojos perros fumaban sus pipas y un olor de cuero
  caliente
ponía grises los labios redondos de los que vomitaban en
  las esquinas.
Y llegaban largos alaridos por el Sur de la noche seca.
Era que la luna quemaba con sus bujías el falo de los
  caballos.
Un sastre especialista en púrpura
había encerrado a las tres santas mujeres
y les enseñaba una calavera por los vidrios de la ventana.
Los tres niños en el arrabal rodeaban a un camello
  blanco
que lloraba porque al alba
tenía que pasar sin remedio por el ojo de una aguja.
¡Oh cruz! ¡Oh clavos! ¡Oh espina!
¡Oh espina clavada en el hueso hasta que se oxiden los
  planetas!
Como nadie volvía la cabeza, el cielo pudo desnudarse.
Entonces se oyó la voz y los fariseos dijeron:
Esa maldita vaca tiene las tetas llenas de leche.
La muchedumbre cerraba las puertas

Crucifixion

The moon could rest in the end along the pure white
    curve of the horses.
A violent beam of light that escaped from a wound
projected the instant of a dead child's circumcision on
    the sky.

Blood flowed down the mountain and angels looked
    for it,
but the chalices became wind and finally filled the shoes.
Crippled dogs puffed on their pipes and the odor of hot
    leather
grayed the round lips of those who vomited on street
    corners.
And long southern howls arrived with the arid night.
It was the moon burning the horses' phallus with its
    candles.
A tailor, who specialized in purple,
had locked up three saintly women
and was showing them a skull through the window
    glass.
In the borough, three boys circled a white camel
that wept because at dawn
there was no other way except through the needle's eye.
Oh, cross! Oh, nails! Oh, thorn!
Oh, thorn driven to the bone until the planets rust to
    pieces!
Since no one turned to look, the sky could undress.
Then the great voice was heard, and the pharisees said:
That wicked cow has teats full of milk.
The multitude locked their doors

143.

y la lluvia bajaba por las calles decidida a mojar el
   corazón
mientras la tarde se puso turbia de latidos y leñadores
y la oscura ciudad agonizaba bajo el martillo de los
   carpinteros.
Esa maldita vaca
tiene las tetas llenas de perdigones,
dijeron los fariseos azules.
Pero la sangre mojó sus pies y los espíritus inmundos
estrellaban ampollas de laguna sobre las paredes del
   templo.
Se supo el momento preciso de la salvación de nuestra
   vida.
Porque la luna lavó con agua
las quemaduras de los caballos
y no la niña viva que callaron en la arena.
Entonces salieron los fríos cantando sus canciones
y las ranas encendieron sus lumbres en la doble orilla del
   río.
Esa maldita vaca, maldita, maldita, maldita,
no nos dejará dormir, dijeron los fariseos,
y se alejaron a sus casas por el tumulto de la calle
dando empujones a los borrachos y escupiendo la sal de
   los sacrificios
mientras la sangre los seguía con un balido de cordero.

Fue entonces
y la tierra despertó arrojando temblorosos ríos de polilla.

Nueva York, 18 de octubre 1929

and rain flowed down the streets, determined to drench
  their hearts
while the evening clouded over with heartbeats and
  woodcutters
and the darkened city agonized under the carpenters'
  hammer.
That wicked cow
has teats full of bird shot,
said the blue pharisees.
But blood drenched their feet and unclean spirits
splattered drops of blistered ponds on the temple walls.
Someone knew the precise moment that our lives would
  be saved
because the moon washed the burns
of the horses with water
and not the living girl they silenced in the sand.
Then the chills went out singing their songs
and frogs ignited fires on the river's double shore.
That wicked cow, wicked, wicked, wicked,
won't let us sleep, said the pharisees,
and they withdrew to their houses through the riotous
  street,
pushing drunks aside and spitting sacrificial salt
while the blood followed them like a bleating lamb.

That's how it was
and the awakened earth cast off trembling rivers of
  moths.

New York, October 18, 1929

145.

VIII

DOS ODAS

A mi editor, Armando Guibert

VIII
TWO ODES

To my publisher, Armando Guibert

Grito hacia Roma
(Desde la torre del Chrysler Building)

Manzanas levemente heridas
por finos espadines de plata,
nubes rasgadas por una mano de coral
que lleva en el dorso una almendra de fuego,
peces de arsénico como tiburones,
tiburones como gotas de llanto para cegar una multitud,
rosas que hieren
y agujas instaladas en los caños de la sangre,
mundos enemigos y amores cubiertos de gusanos
caerán sobre ti. Caerán sobre la gran cúpula
que unta de aceite las lenguas militares,
donde un hombre se orina en una deslumbrante paloma
y escupe carbón machacado
rodeado de miles de campanillas.

Porque ya no hay quien reparta el pan y el vino,
ni quien cultive hierbas en la boca del muerto,
ni quien abra los linos del reposo,
ni quien llore por las heridas de los elefantes.
No hay más que un millón de herreros
forjando cadenas para los niños que han de venir.
No hay más que un millón de carpinteros
que hacen ataúdes sin cruz.
No hay más que un gentío de lamentos
que se abren las ropas en espera de las balas.
El hombre que desprecia la paloma debía hablar,
debía gritar desnudo entre las columnas
y ponerse una inyección para adquirir la lepra
y llorar un llanto tan terrible
que disolviera sus anillos y sus teléfonos de diamante.

148.

Cry to Rome
(From the Tower of the Chrysler Building)

Apples barely grazed
by slender, silver rapiers,
clouds torn apart by a coral hand
that carries a fiery almond on its back,
arsenic fish like sharks,
sharks like wailing drops that blind the masses,
roses that wound
and needles that lace the blood's plumbing,
enemy worlds and loves covered with worms
will fall on you. Will fall on the great dome
that anoints the military tongues with oil,
where a man pisses on a dazzling dove
and spits pulverized coal
encircled by thousands of hand bells.

Because there is no one to bestow the bread or the wine,
or make grass grow in the mouths of the dead,
or spread the linen of rest and peace,
or weep for the wounded elephants.
There are only a million blacksmiths
who forge chains for tomorrow's children.
Only a million carpenters
who make coffins with no cross.
Only a crowd of laments
unbuttoning their clothes, waiting for the bullets.
The man who scorns the dove should have spoken,
screamed naked between the columns,
and injected himself with leprosy
and shed tears terrible enough
to dissolve his rings and diamond telephones.

149.

Pero el hombre vestido de blanco
ignora el misterio de la espiga,
ignora el gemido de la parturienta,
ignora que Cristo puede dar agua todavía,
ignora que la moneda quema el beso de prodigio
y da la sangre del cordero al pico idiota del faisán.

Los maestros enseñan a los niños
una luz maravillosa que viene del monte;
pero lo que llega es una reunión de cloacas
donde gritan las oscuras ninfas del cólera.
Los maestros señalan con devoción las enormes cúpulas
    sahumadas;
pero debajo de las estatuas no hay amor,
no hay amor bajo los ojos de cristal definitivo.
El amor está en las carnes desgarradas por la sed,
en la choza diminuta que lucha con la inundación;
el amor está en los fosos donde luchan las sierpes del
    hambre,
en el triste mar que mece los cadáveres de las gaviotas
y en el oscurísimo beso punzante debajo de las
    almohadas.
Pero el viejo de las manos traslúcidas
dirá: Amor, amor, amor,
aclamado por millones de moribundos;
dirá: Amor, amor, amor,
entre el tisú estremecido de ternura;
dirá: Paz, paz, paz,
entre el tirite de cuchillos y melenas de dinamita;
dirá: Amor, amor, amor,
hasta que se le pongan de plata los labios.

Mientras tanto, mientras tanto, ¡ay!, mientras tanto,
los negros que sacan las escupideras,

150.

But the man dressed in white
ignores the mystery of the wheat ear,
ignores the moans of a woman giving birth,
ignores the fact that Christ can still give water,
ignores the money that burns the prodigy's kiss
and gives the blood of the lamb to the pheasant's idiot
   beak.

The schoolteachers show the children
a marvelous light coming from the mountain;
but what arrives is a junction of sewers
where cholera's nymphs scream in the shadows.
The teachers point devoutly to the enormous domes
   filled with burning incense;
but beneath the statues there is no love,
no love beneath the final crystal eyes.
Love is in the flesh shredded by thirst,
in the tiny thatched hut struggling against the flood;
love is in the pits where the serpents of famine writhe,
in the sad sea where the dead gulls drift
and in the obscurest kiss bristling beneath the pillows.
But the old man with translucent hands
will say: Love, love, love,
acclaimed by millions of the dying;
he will say: Love, love, love,
amidst the gold lamé that trembles with tenderness;
he will say: Peace, peace, peace,
among the shivering of knives and long hair of
   dynamite;
he will say: Love, love, love,
until his lips have turned to silver.

Meanwhile, yes, meanwhile
the blacks who remove the spittoons,

151.

los muchachos que tiemblan bajo el terror pálido de los
   directores,
las mujeres ahogadas en aceites minerales,
la muchedumbre de martillo, de violín o de nube,
ha de gritar aunque le estrellen los sesos en el muro,
ha de gritar frente a las cúpulas,
ha de gritar loca de fuego,
ha de gritar loca de nieve,
ha de gritar con la cabeza llena de excremento,
ha de gritar como todas las noches juntas,
ha de gritar con voz tan desgarrada
hasta que las ciudades tiemblen como niñas
y rompan las prisiones del aceite y la música.
Porque queremos el pan nuestro de cada día,
flor de aliso y perenne ternura desgranada,
porque queremos que se cumpla la voluntad de la Tierra
que da sus frutos para todos.

the boys who tremble beneath the pallid terror of
    executives,
the women who drown in mineral oil,
the multitudes with their hammers, violins, or clouds—
they'll scream even if they bash their brains against the
    wall,
scream in front of the domes,
scream driven crazy by fire,
scream driven crazy by snow,
scream with their heads full of excrement,
scream as if all the nights converged,
scream with such a heartrending voice
until the cities tremble like little girls
and knock down the prisons of oil and music.
Because we demand our daily bread,
alder in bloom and perennially harvested tenderness,
because we demand that Earth's will be done,
that its fruits be offered to everyone.

Oda a Walt Whitman

Por el East River y el Bronx
los muchachos cantaban enseñando sus cinturas,
con la rueda, el aceite, el cuero y el martillo.
Noventa mil mineros sacaban la plata de las rocas
y los niños dibujaban escaleras y perspectivas.

Pero ninguno se dormía,
ninguno quería ser río,
ninguno amaba las hojas grandes,
ninguno la lengua azul de la playa.

Por el East River y el Queensboro
los muchachos luchaban con la industria,
y los judíos vendían al fauno del río
la rosa de la circuncisión
y el cielo desembocaba por los puentes y los tejados
manadas de bisontes empujadas por el viento.

Pero ninguno se detenía,
ninguno quería ser nube,
ninguno buscaba los helechos
ni la rueda amarilla del tamboril.

Cuando la luna salga
las poleas rodarán para turbar el cielo;
un límite de agujas cercará la memoria
y los ataúdes se llevarán a los que no trabajan.

Nueva York de cieno,
Nueva York de alambre y de muerte.

154.

Ode to Walt Whitman

By the East River and the Bronx
boys were singing, exposing their waists,
with the wheel, with oil, leather, and the hammer.
Ninety thousand miners taking silver from the rocks
and children drawing stairs and perspectives.

But none of them could sleep,
none of them wanted to be the river,
none of them loved the huge leaves
or the shoreline's blue tongue.

By the East River and the Queensboro
boys were battling with industry
and the Jews sold to the river faun
the rose of circumcision,
and over bridges and rooftops, the mouth of the sky
    emptied
herds of bison driven by the wind.

But none of them paused,
none of them wanted to be a cloud,
none of them looked for ferns
or the yellow wheel of the tambourine.

As soon as the moon rises
the pulleys will spin to alter the sky;
a border of needles will besiege memory
and the hearses will bear away those who don't work.

New York, mire,
New York, wire and death.

155.

¿Qué ángel llevas oculto en la mejilla?
¿Qué voz perfecta dirá las verdades del trigo?
¿Quién el sueño terrible de tus anémonas manchadas?

Ni un solo momento, viejo hermoso Walt Whitman,
he dejado de ver tu barba llena de mariposas,
ni tus hombros de pana gastados por la luna,
ni tus muslos de Apolo virginal,
ni tu voz como una columna de ceniza;
anciano hermoso como la niebla,
que gemías igual que un pájaro
con el sexo atravesado por una aguja.
Enemigo del sátiro,
enemigo de la vid
y amante de los cuerpos bajo la burda tela.

Ni un solo momento, hermosura viril
que en montes de carbón, anuncios y ferrocarriles,
soñabas ser un río y dormir como un río
con aquel camarada que pondría en tu pecho
un pequeño dolor de ignorante leopardo.

Ni un solo momento, Adán de sangre, Macho,
hombre solo en el mar, viejo hermoso Walt Whitman,
porque por las azoteas,
agrupados en los bares,
saliendo en racimos de las alcantarillas,
temblando entre las piernas de los chauffeurs
o girando en las plataformas del ajenjo,
los maricas, Walt Whitman, te señalan.

¡También ése! ¡También! Y se despeñan
sobre tu barba luminosa y casta,
rubios del norte, negros de la arena,

What angel is hidden in your cheek?
Whose perfect voice will sing the truths of wheat?
Who, the terrible dream of your bruised anemones?

Not for a moment, Walt Whitman, lovely old man,
have I failed to see your beard full of butterflies,
nor your corduroy shoulders frayed by the moon,
nor your thighs as pure as Apollo's,
nor your voice like a column of ash;
old man, beautiful as the mist,
you moaned like a bird
with its sex pierced by a needle.
Enemy of the satyr,
enemy of the vine,
and lover of bodies beneath rough cloth . . .

Not for a moment, virile beauty,
who among mountains of coal, billboards, and railroads,
dreamed of becoming a river and sleeping like a river
with that comrade who would place in your breast
the small ache of an ignorant leopard.

Not for a moment, Adam of blood, Macho,
man alone at sea, Walt Whitman, lovely old man,
because on penthouse roofs,
gathered at bars,
emerging in bunches from the sewers,
trembling between the legs of chauffeurs,
or spinning on dance floors wet with absinthe,
the faggots, Walt Whitman, point you out.

He's one, too! That's right! And they land
on your luminous chaste beard,
blonds from the north, blacks from the sands,

157.

muchedumbre de gritos y ademanes
como los gatos y como las serpientes,
los maricas, Walt Whitman, los maricas,
turbios de lágrimas, carne para fusta,
bota o mordisco de los domadores.

¡También ése! ¡También! Dedos teñidos
apuntan a la orilla de tu sueño,
cuando el amigo come tu manzana
con un leve sabor de gasolina
y el sol canta por los ombligos
de los muchachos que juegan bajo los puentes.

Pero tú no buscabas los ojos arañados,
ni el pantano oscurísimo donde sumergen a los niños,
ni la saliva helada,
ni las curvas heridas como panza de sapo
que llevan los maricas en coches y en terrazas
mientras la luna los azota por las esquinas del terror.

Tú buscabas un desnudo que fuera como un río.
Toro y sueño que junte la rueda con el alga,
padre de tu agonía, camelia de tu muerte,
y gimiera en las llamas de tu ecuador oculto.

Porque es justo que el hombre no busque su deleite
en la selva de sangre de la mañana próxima.
El cielo tiene playas donde evitar la vida
y hay cuerpos que no deben repetirse en la aurora.

crowds of howls and gestures,
like cats or like snakes,
the faggots, Walt Whitman, the faggots,
clouded with tears, flesh for the whip,
the boot, or the teeth of the lion tamers.

He's one, too! That's right! Stained fingers
point to the shore of your dream
when a friend eats your apple
with a slight taste of gasoline
and the sun sings in the navels
of boys who play under bridges.

But you didn't look for scratched eyes,
nor the darkest swamp where someone submerges
    children,
nor frozen saliva,
nor the curves slit open like a toad's belly
that the faggots wear in cars and on terraces
while the moon lashes them on the street corners of
    terror.

You looked for a naked body like a river.
Bull and dream who would join wheel with seaweed,
father of your agony, camellia of your death,
who would groan in the blaze of your hidden equator.

Because it's all right if a man doesn't look for his delight
in tomorrow morning's jungle of blood.
The sky has shores where life is avoided
and there are bodies that shouldn't repeat themselves in
    the dawn.

159.

Agonía, agonía, sueño, fermento y sueño.
Este es el mundo, amigo, agonía, agonía.
Los muertos se descomponen bajo el reloj de las
    ciudades,
la guerra pasa llorando con un millón de ratas grises,
los ricos dan a sus queridas
pequeños moribundos iluminados,
y la vida no es noble, ni buena, ni sagrada.

Puede el hombre, si quiere, conducir su deseo
por vena de coral o celeste desnudo.
Mañana los amores serán rocas y el Tiempo
una brisa que viene dormida por las ramas.

Por eso no levanto mi voz, viejo Walt Whitman,
contra el niño que escribe
nombre de niña en su almohada,
ni contra el muchacho que se viste de novia
en la oscuridad del ropero,
ni contra los solitarios de los casinos
que beben con asco el agua de la prostitución,
ni contra los hombres de mirada verde
que aman al hombre y queman sus labios en silencio.

Pero sí contra vosotros, maricas de las ciudades,
de carne tumefacta y pensamiento inmundo.
Madres de lodo. Arpías. Enemigos sin sueño
del Amor que reparte coronas de alegría.

Contra vosotros siempre, que dais a los muchachos
gotas de sucia muerte con amargo veneno.
Contra vosotros siempre,
Fairies de Norteamérica,
Pájaros de La Habana,
Jotos de Méjico,

160.

Agony, agony, dream, ferment and dream.
This is the world, my friend, agony, agony.
Bodies decompose beneath the city clocks,
war passes by in tears, followed by a million gray rats,
the rich give their mistresses
small illuminated dying things,
and life is neither noble, nor good, nor sacred.

Man is able, if he wishes, to guide his desire
through a vein of coral or a heavenly naked body.
Tomorrow, loves will become stones, and Time
a breeze that drowses in the branches.

That's why I don't raise my voice, old Walt Whitman,
against the little boy who writes
the name of a girl on his pillow,
nor against the boy who dresses as a bride
in the darkness of the wardrobe,
nor against the solitary men in casinos
who drink prostitution's water with revulsion,
nor against the men with that green look in their eyes
who love other men and burn their lips in silence.

But yes against you, urban faggots,
tumescent flesh and unclean thoughts.
Mothers of mud. Harpies. Sleepless enemies
of the love that bestows crowns of joy.

Always against you, who give boys
drops of foul death with bitter poison.
Always against you,
Fairies of North America,
Pájaros of Havana,
Jotos of Mexico,

161.

Sarasas de Cádiz,
Apios de Sevilla,
Cancos de Madrid,
Floras de Alicante,
Adelaidas de Portugal.

¡Maricas de todo el mundo, asesinos de palomas!
Esclavos de la mujer. Perras de sus tocadores.
Abiertos en las plazas con fiebre de abanico
o emboscados en yertos paisajes de cicuta.

¡No haya cuartel! La muerte
mana de vuestros ojos
y agrupa flores grises en la orilla del cieno.
¡No haya cuartel! ¡¡Alerta!!
Que los confundidos, los puros,
los clásicos, los señalados, los suplicantes
os cierren las puertas de la bacanal.

Y tú, bello Walt Whitman, duerme a orillas del Hudson
con la barba hacia el polo y las manos abiertas.
Arcilla blanda o nieve, tu lengua está llamando
camaradas que velen tu gacela sin cuerpo.

Duerme: no queda nada.
Una danza de muros agita las praderas
y América se anega de máquinas y llanto.
Quiero que el aire fuerte de la noche más honda
quite flores y letras del arco donde duermes
y un niño negro anuncie a los blancos del oro
la llegada del reino de la espiga.

Sarasas of Cádiz,
Apios of Seville,
Cancos of Madrid,
Floras of Alicante,
Adelaidas of Portugal.

Faggots of the world, murderers of doves!
Slaves of women. Their bedroom bitches.
Opening in public squares like feverish fans
or ambushed in rigid hemlock landscapes.

No quarter given! Death
spills from your eyes
and gathers gray flowers at the mire's edge.
No quarter given! Attention!
Let the confused, the pure,
the classical, the celebrated, the supplicants
close the doors of the bacchanal to you.

And you, lovely Walt Whitman, stay asleep on the
    Hudson's banks
with your beard toward the pole, openhanded.
Soft clay or snow, your tongue calls for
comrades to keep watch over your unbodied gazelle.

Sleep on, nothing remains.
Dancing walls stir the prairies
and America drowns itself in machinery and lament.
I want the powerful air from the deepest night
to blow away flowers and inscriptions from the arch
    where you sleep,
and a black child to inform the gold-craving whites
that the kingdom of grain has arrived.

163.

IX

HUÍDA DE

NUEVA YORK

(Dos valses hacia

la civilización)

IX

FLIGHT FROM

NEW YORK

(Two Waltzes toward

Civilization)

[García Lorca, *Self-portrait with Fabulous
Animal in Black*, 1929–1931]

Pequeño vals vienés

En Viena hay diez muchachas,
un hombro donde solloza la muerte
y un bosque de palomas disecadas.
Hay un fragmento de la mañana
en el museo de la escarcha.
Hay un salón con mil ventanas.

¡Ay, ay, ay, ay!
Toma este vals con la boca cerrada.

Este vals, este vals, este vals,
de sí, de muerte y de coñac
que moja su cola en el mar.

Te quiero, te quiero, te quiero,
con la butaca y el libro muerto,
por el melancólico pasillo,
en el oscuro desván del lirio,
en nuestra cama de la luna
y en la danza que sueña la tortuga.

¡Ay, ay, ay, ay!
Toma este vals de quebrada cintura.

En Viena hay cuatro espejos
donde juegan tu boca y los ecos.
Hay una muerte para piano
que pinta de azul a los muchachos.
Hay mendigos por los tejados.
Hay frescas guirnaldas de llanto.

166.

Little Viennese Waltz

In Vienna there are ten little girls,
a shoulder for death to cry on,
and a forest of dried pigeons.
There is a fragment of tomorrow
in the museum of winter frost.
There is a thousand-windowed dance hall.

Ay, ay, ay, ay!
Take this close-mouthed waltz.

Little waltz, little waltz, little waltz,
of itself, of death, and of brandy
that dips its tail in the sea.

I love you, I love you, I love you,
with the armchair and the book of death,
down the melancholy hallway,
in the iris's darkened garret,
in our bed that was once the moon's bed,
and in that dance the turtle dreamed of.

Ay, ay, ay, ay!
Take this broken-waisted waltz.

In Vienna there are four mirrors
in which your mouth and the echoes play.
There is a death for piano
that paints the little boys blue.
There are beggars on the roof.
There are fresh garlands of tears.

167.

¡Ay, ay, ay, ay!
Toma este vals que se muere en mis brazos.

Porque te quiero, te quiero, amor mío,
en el desván donde juegan los niños,
soñando viejas luces de Hungría
por los rumores de la tarde tibia,
viendo ovejas y lirios de nieve
por el silencio oscuro de tu frente.

¡Ay, ay, ay, ay!
Toma este vals del "Te quiero siempre."

En Viena bailaré contigo
con un disfraz que tenga
cabeza de río.
¡Mira qué orillas tengo de jacintos!
Dejaré mi boca entre tus piernas,
mi alma en fotografías y azucenas,
y en las ondas oscuras de tu andar
quiero, amor mío, amor mío, dejar,
violín y sepulcro, las cintas del vals.

Aye, ay, ay, ay!
Take this waltz that dies in my arms.

Because I love you, I love you, my love,
in the attic where the children play,
dreaming ancient lights of Hungary
through the noise, the balmy afternoon,
seeing sheep and irises of snow
through the dark silence of your forehead.

Ay, ay, ay, ay!
Take this "I will always love you" waltz.

In Vienna I will dance with you
in a costume with
a river's head.
See how the hyacinths line my banks!
I will leave my mouth between your legs,
my soul in photographs and lilies,
and in the dark wake of your footsteps,
my love, my love, I will have to leave
violin and grave, the waltzing ribbons.

Vals en las ramas

Cayó una hoja
y dos
y tres.
Por la luna nadaba un pez.
El agua duerme una hora
y el mar blanco duerme cien.
La dama
estaba muerta en la rama.
La monja
cantaba dentro de la toronja.
La niña
iba por el pino a la piña.
Y el pino
buscaba la plumilla del trino.
Pero el ruiseñor
lloraba sus heridas alrededor.
Y yo también
porque cayó una hoja
y dos
y tres.
Y una cabeza de cristal
y un violín de papel.
Y la nieve podría con el mundo
si la nieve durmiera un mes,
y las ramas luchaban con el mundo,
una a una,
dos a dos
y tres a tres.
¡Oh duro marfil de carnes invisibles!
¡Oh golfo sin hormigas del amanecer!
Con el muuu de las ramas,

Waltz in the Branches

One leaf fell,
a second
and a third.
A fish swam on the moon.
The water sleeps for only an hour,
but the white sea sleeps for a hundred.
There is a dead lady
in the branch of the tree.
The nun in her habit
sang inside the pomegranate.
This girl of mine
reached the pinecone from the pine.
And the pine went along
to look for the tiny feather's song.
But the wounded nightingale cried
throughout the countryside.
And I did too,
because the first leaf fell,
a second
and a third.
And a head of crystal
and a paper fiddle.
And the snow could make its way in the world,
if the snow slept for a month,
and the branches wrestled with the world,
one by one,
two by two
and three by three.
Oh, the hard ivory of invisible flesh!
Oh, the dawn's abyss with no ants!
With the swish of the trees,

con el ay de las damas,
con el croo de las ranas
y el gloo amarillo de la miel.
Llegará un torso de sombra
coronado de laurel.
Será el cielo para el viento
duro como una pared
y las ramas desgajadas
se irán bailando con él.
Una a una
alrededor de la luna,
dos a dos
alrededor del sol,
y tres a tres
para que los marfiles se duerman bien.

with the sighs of the ladies,
with the croaking frogs
and the honey's yellow glug.
A shadow's torso will arrive,
wearing a laurel crown.
For the wind, the sky will
be as hard as a wall
and all the downed branches
will leave as they dance.
One by one
around the moon,
two by two
around the sun,
and three by three
let the pieces of ivory sleep.

X

EL POETA
LLEGA
A LA HABANA

A don Fernando Ortiz

X

THE POET

ARRIVES

IN HAVANA

To Don Fernando Ortiz

[Lorca in Havana, June 8, 1930]

Son de negros en Cuba

Cuando llegue la luna llena iré a Santiago de Cuba,
iré a Santiago
en un coche de agua negra.
Iré a Santiago.
Cantarán los techos de palmera.
Iré a Santiago.
Cuando la palma quiere ser cigüeña,
iré a Santiago.
Y cuando quiere ser medusa el plátano,
iré a Santiago.
Iré a Santiago
con la rubia cabeza de Fonseca.
Iré a Santiago.
Y con el rosa de Romeo y Julieta
iré a Santiago.
Mar de papel y plata de monedas.
Iré a Santiago.
¡Oh Cuba! ¡Oh ritmo de semillas secas!
Iré a Santiago.
¡Oh cintura caliente y gota de madera!
Iré a Santiago.
Arpa de troncos vivos. Caimán. Flor de tabaco.
Iré a Santiago.
Siempre he dicho que yo iría a Santiago
en un coche de agua negra.
Iré a Santiago.
Brisa y alcohol en las ruedas,
iré a Santiago.
Mi coral en la tiniebla,

Blacks Dancing to Cuban Rhythms

As soon as the full moon rises, I'm going to Santiago,
   Cuba,
I'm going to Santiago
in a coach of black water.
I'm going to Santiago.
The palm trees will sing above the rooftops.
I'm going to Santiago.
When the palm wants to be a stork,
I'm going to Santiago.
When the banana tree wants to be a sea wasp,
I'm going to Santiago.
I'm going to Santiago
with Fonseca's blond head.
I'm going to Santiago.
And with Romeo and Juliet's rose
I'm going to Santiago.
Paper sea and silver coins.
I'm going to Santiago.
Oh, Cuba, oh, rhythm of dried seeds!
I'm going to Santiago.
Oh, fiery waist, oh, drop of wood!
I'm going to Santiago.
Harp of living tree trunks. Crocodile. Tobacco plant in
   bloom!
I'm going to Santiago.
I always said I'd go to Santiago
in a coach of black water.
I'm going to Santiago.
Wind and rum on the wheels,
I'm going to Santiago.
My coral in the darkness,

177.

iré a Santiago.
El mar ahogado en la arena,
iré a Santiago.
Calor blanco, fruta muerta,
iré a Santiago.
¡Oh bovino frescor de cañavera!
¡Oh Cuba! ¡Oh curva de suspiro y barro!
Iré a Santiago.

La Habana, abril 1930

I'm going to Santiago.
The sea drowned in the sand,
I'm going to Santiago.
White heat, rotting fruit,
I'm going to Santiago.
Oh, the bovine coolness of sugar cane!
Oh, Cuba! Oh, curve of sigh and clay!
I'm going to Santiago.

Havana, April 1930

LECTURE:
A POET IN
NEW YORK

Translated by Christopher Maurer

The untitled autograph manuscript of this lecture in the archives of the Fundación Federico García Lorca, Madrid, does not appear to be a final draft. This lecture was first given in Madrid (March 1932) and repeated in other cities of Spain, Argentina, and Uruguay. Lorca had delayed publication of *Poet in New York*, preferring to "make it known in the form of a lecture. I will read poems and explain how they came to be; that is, I will read the book and analyze it at the same time" (from an interview of 1933, *OC*, Vol. III, p. 556). I have followed the transcription of Eutimio Martín, ed., *Poeta en Nueva York / Tierra y luna* (Barcelona: Ariel, 1981), pp. 305–17, checking it against a photocopy of the original.

[Lorca at Columbia, October 1929]

Ladies and gentlemen:

Whenever I speak before a large group I always think I must have opened the wrong door. Some friendly hands have given me a shove, and here I am. Half of us wander around completely lost amid drop curtains, painted trees, and tin fountains, and just when we think we have found our room, or our circle of lukewarm sun, we meet an alligator who swallows us alive, or . . . an audience, as I have. And today the only show I can offer you is some bitter, living poetry. Perhaps I can lash its eyes open for you.

I have said "A Poet in New York" when I ought to have said "New York in a Poet." The poet is me, purely and simply: a poet who has neither talent nor genius, but who can sometimes escape through the murky edge of the looking glass of day more quickly than most children. A poet who comes to this auditorium wanting to imagine that he is back in his room, and that you are my friends; for there can be no written poetry unless eyes are enslaved to the obscure line, and no spoken poetry unless ears are docile and friendly. That way, the word can body forth and carry blood to the speaker's lips and sky to the listener's brow.

In any event, one must speak clearly. I have not come here to entertain you: I do not want to, and simply couldn't care less. I am here to fight. Fight hand to hand against a complacent mass, for I am not about to give a lecture but a poetry reading—my flesh, my joy, and my feelings— and I need to defend myself from the huge dragon out there who could eat me alive with three hundred yawns of his three hundred disappointed heads. And that is what I mean by fighting. Now that I have come, and have broken my long poetic silence for a moment,[1] I badly want

[1] Between 1928, the year the *Gypsy Ballads* was published, and 1932, the year he gave this lecture for the first time, García Lorca had published only one book, *Poema del cante jondo*, written many years earlier, in 1921.

to communicate with you. Not to give you honey (I have none), but sand or hemlock or salt water. Hand-to-hand fighting, and it does not matter if I am defeated.

Let us agree that one of man's most beautiful postures is that of St. Sebastian.[2]

Well then, before reading poems aloud to so many people, the first thing one must do is invoke the *duende*. This is the only way all of you will succeed at the hard task of understanding metaphors as soon as they arise, without depending on intelligence or on a critical apparatus, and be able to capture, as fast as it is read, the rhythmic design of the poem.[3] For the quality of a poem can never be judged on just one reading, especially not poems like these which are full of what I call "poetic facts"[4] that respond to a purely poetic logic and follow the constructs of emotion and of poetic architecture. Poems like these are not likely to be understood without the cordial help of the *duende*.

But in any case, I, as a man and as a poet, have a great rain cape, a cape that says "It's *your* fault, not mine," a cape which I hang on the shoulders of anyone who comes

[2] To both García Lorca and his friend Salvador Dalí, St. Sebastian was a complex, contradictory symbol of vulnerability, artistic objectivity, and the cool conquest of one's own emotion. See Dalí's prose poem "Sant Sebastià" in Ian Gibson, pp. 612–17; Lorca's 1926 letter to Jorge Guillén, where he argues that true poetry is "love, effort and *renunciation* (St. Sebastian)" (*OC*, Vol. III, p. 892); and his drawing of the saint (*OC*, Vol. III, p. 1052).

[3] Parts of this introductory section are missing in the manuscript, and other parts were crossed out at an unknown date. In the earliest readings of the lecture, Lorca may have explained in detail his concept of *duende*. This material was probably removed from the version read in Buenos Aires and Montevideo (1933–34) because by then it had been incorporated into a new lecture entitled "Play and Theory of the *Duende*" (English translation by C. Maurer in *Deep Song and Other Prose* [N.Y.: New Directions, 1980], pp. 42–53).

[4] "Hecho poético" is Lorca's term for a poetic image which, unlike the normal metaphor based on analogy, has no apparent logical explanation. See his lecture entitled "Imaginación, inspiración, evasión" (1928–30), where he gives as an example two lines from *The Gypsy Ballads*: "Green, I want you green, / green wind, green boughs" (*Conferencias*, Vol. II, p. 23).

to me for an explanation. As for me, I can explain nothing, but stammer with the fire that burns inside me and the life that has been bestowed on me.

I will not tell you what New York is like *from the outside*, because New York, like Moscow (two antagonistic cities), is the subject of countless descriptive books. Nor will I narrate a voyage. What I will give is my lyrical reaction, with sincerity and simplicity: two qualities that come with difficulty to intellectuals, but easily to the poet. To come here, I have had to overcome my poetic modesty.

The two elements the traveler first captures in the big city are extrahuman architecture and furious rhythm. Geometry and anguish. At first glance, the rhythm may be confused with gaiety, but when you look more closely at the mechanism of social life and the painful slavery of both men and machines, you see that it is nothing but a kind of typical, empty anguish that makes even crime and gangs forgivable means of escape.

The sharp-edged buildings rise to the sky with no desire for either clouds or glory. The angles and edges of Gothic architecture surge from the hearts of the dead and buried, but these climb coldly skyward with a beauty that has no roots and reveals no longing, stupidly complacent and utterly unable to transcend or conquer, as does spiritual architecture, the perpetually inferior intentions of the architect. There is nothing more poetic and terrible than the skyscrapers' battle with the heavens that cover them. Snow, rain, and mist highlight, drench, or conceal the vast towers, but those towers, hostile to mystery and blind to any sort of play, shear off the rain's tresses and shine their three thousand swords through the soft swan of the fog.

It only takes a few days to realize that this immense world has no roots, and to understand why the seer Edgar

185.

Poe had to hug mystery so close to him and let friendly intoxication boil in his veins.[5]

A solitary wanderer, I evoked my childhood like this. [He reads the poem "1910 (Intermezzo)."]

In the following little poem, I wandered alone, exhausted by the rhythm of the huge electric billboards in Times Square. I fled from the great army of windows, where not a single person has the time to watch a cloud or converse with one of those delicate breezes stubbornly sent by the unanswered sea. Poem: "Cut Down by the Sky" ["After a Walk"].

But you have to go out and conquer the city, and not surrender to lyrical reactions without having rubbed shoulders with the crowds on the avenues and the medley of people from all over the world.[6]

So I take to the streets, and I encounter the blacks. New York is a meeting place for every race in the world, but the Chinese, Armenians, Russians, and Germans remain foreigners. So does everyone except the blacks. There is no doubt but that the blacks exercise great influence in North America, and, no matter what anyone says, they are the most delicate, most spiritual element in that world. Because they believe, because they hope and they sing, and because they have an exquisite, religious indolence that

[5] Lorca's friend Sofía Megwinoff, who had the unenviable task of tutoring him in English, remembers his fascination with "Annabel Lee" and "The Bells": "He was hypnotized by the rhythm. He understood nothing. But he kept time with his hand . . . and hummed . . . and repeated this or that melodious snatch of the poem . . . He imitated my voice and was absorbed by the sound, and there was a look of veneration on his face. He brought me the book every day, so that I could read it to him" (Daniel Eisenberg, "Cuatro pesquisas lorquianas," *Thesaurus* [Bogotá] XXX [1975], p. 15; my translation).

[6] Struck from the manuscript: "And I take to the streets. And one night in the deathly Armenian neighborhood, I hear these voices behind the wall, talking about a murder" [text of "Murder"].

redeems them of all their dangerous, present–day concerns.

If you travel through the Bronx or Brooklyn, where the blond Americans live, you sense a certain deafness: people who love walls that can shut out the stray glance; a clock in every house; a God glimpsed only by the soles of his feet. But in the black neighborhood there is something like a constant exchange of smiles; a deep earth tremor that rusts the nickel columns; the wounded little boy who, if you stare at him long enough, will offer you his apple pie.

In the morning I would often walk down from the university where I lived, and I was no longer the frightening "Mister Lorca" of my professors, but the strange "sleepy boy"[7] of the waitresses. And, wanting to find out what the blacks were thinking, I watched them dance, for dance is the unique, poignant way they express their feelings and their pain. I wrote this poem: "Standards and Paradise of the Blacks."

But I still hadn't gotten it right. What I had before my eyes was neither an aesthetic norm nor a blue paradise. What I looked at, strolled through, dreamed about, was the most important black city in the world, Harlem, where obscenity has an accent of innocence that turns it into something disturbing and religious. A neighborhood of reddish houses, full of player pianos and radios and cinemas, but with the *mistrust* that characterizes the race. Doors half closed, black-quartz children afraid of the rich people from Park Avenue, gramophones whose song is suddenly interrupted, the wait for the enemies who could come down the East River and point out exactly where the idols are sleeping. I wanted to write *the* poem of the black race in North America, and to show the pain the blacks feel to be black in a contrary world. They are slaves of all the white

7 "Sleepe boy" in the original. The meaning is not quite clear.

man's inventions and machines, perpetually afraid that someday they will forget how to light the gas stove or steer the automobile or fasten the starched collar, afraid of driving a fork through an eye. I mean that these inventions are not theirs. The blacks live on borrowed things, and the black fathers have to maintain strict discipline at home lest their women and children adore the gramophone record or eat the tires of automobiles.

And yet any visitor can easily see that, for all their ebullience, they yearn to be a nation, and even though they occasionally make theater out of themselves, in the depths of their spirit they are incorruptible. In one cabaret—Smalls Paradise[8]—whose dancing audience was as black, wet, and grainy as a tin of caviar, I saw a naked dancer shuddering convulsively under an invisible rain of fire. But while everyone shouted as though believing her to be possessed by the rhythm, I stared into her eyes and, just for a second, felt her reserve, her remoteness, her inner certainty that she had nothing to do with that admiring audience of Americans and foreigners. All Harlem was like her.

Another time I saw a little black girl riding a bicycle. Nothing could have been more touching: her smoky legs, the balled-up sheep's hair of her head, her cold teeth in the moribund pink of her lips. I stared at her and she stared right back. But my stare was saying: "Little girl, why are you riding a bicycle? Can a little black girl really ride such a thing? Is it yours? Where did you steal it? Do you think you can steer it?" And sure enough, she did a somersault and fell, all legs and wheels, down a gentle slope.

[8] A black night club, less expensive than Connie's Inn and the Cotton Club. "In 1925, Edwin Smalls and his brother Charles moved their famous Fifth Avenue cabaret to 2294 Seventh Avenue. The club is now known as Big Wilt's Smalls Paradise" (M. H. Harris, *A Negro History Tour of Manhattan* [N.Y.: Greenwood, 1968], p. 101).

188.

But every day I protested. I protested to see little black children guillotined by stiff collars, in their suits and violent boots, as they emptied the spittoons of cold men who talked like ducks.

I protested to see so much flesh stolen from paradise and managed by Jews with gelid noses and blotting-paper souls, and I protested against the saddest thing of all, that the blacks do not want to be black, that they invent pomades to take away the delicious curl of their hair, and powders that turn their faces gray, and syrups that fill out their waists and wither the succulent persimmon of their lips.

I protested, and the proof of it is this "Ode to the King of Harlem," the spirit of the black race, a cry of encouragement to those who tremble and search, cautiously and clumsily, for the flesh of the white woman. [Poem.]

And yet the truly savage and frenetic part of New York is not Harlem. In Harlem there is human warmth and the noise of children, and there are homes and grass, and sorrow finds consolation and the wound finds its sweet bandage.

The terrible, cold, cruel part is Wall Street. Rivers of gold flow there from all over the earth, and death comes with it. There, as nowhere else, you feel a total absence of the spirit: herds of men who cannot count past three, herds more who cannot get past six, scorn for pure science and demoniacal respect for the present. And the terrible thing is that the crowd that fills this street believes that the world will always be the same, and that it is their duty to keep that huge machine running, day and night, forever. This is what comes of a Protestant morality that I, as a (thank God) typical Spaniard, found unnerving.

I was lucky enough to see with my own eyes the recent stock-market crash, where they lost several billion dollars, a rabble of dead money that went sliding off into the sea.

189.

Never as then, amid suicides, hysteria, and groups of fainting people, have I felt the sensation of real death, death without hope, death that is nothing but rottenness, for the spectacle was terrifying but devoid of greatness. And I, who come from a country where, as the great father Unamuno said, "at night the earth climbs to the sky,"[9] I felt something like a divine urge to bombard that whole canyon of shadow, where ambulances collected suicides whose hands were full of rings.

That is why I situated this "Dance of Death" in Wall Street. The typical African mask, death which is truly dead, without angels or "Resurrexit"; death totally alien to the spirit, barbarous and primitive as the United States, a country which has never fought, and never will fight, for heaven.[10] [Poem.]

And the crowd! No one can imagine just what a New York crowd is like, except perhaps Walt Whitman, who searched it for solitudes, and T. S. Eliot, who squeezes the crowd like a lemon in his poem, extracting wounded rats, wet hats, and river shades.[11]

But when, in addition, that crowd is drunk, we have one of the most intense spectacles that life can offer.

[9] From Miguel de Unamuno, "En un cementerio de lugar castellano" ("In a Castilian Country Cemetery"), in *Andanzas y visiones españolas*, 1922: "When the sun has slowly come to earth / and the land climbs to the sky, / at the hour of remembrance, / and bells are tolling for prayers and rest, / the rough-hewn stone cross / atop your mud walls / remains, watching like a sleepless guardian / over the dormant countryside" (*Antología poética* [Madrid: Espasa-Calpe, 1968], p. 69).

[10] An allusion to the doctrine of predestination. After the word "Resurrexit," in the manuscript, Lorca deleted: "death of Protestants who think they do not need to fight for heaven, for all is done and will always be the same."

[11] Here, and in his remarks on Coney Island, Lorca seems to be remembering the third section ("The Fire Sermon") of *The Waste Land*: "The river bears no empty bottles, sandwich papers, / Silk handkerchiefs, cardboard boxes, cigarette ends / Or other testimony of summer nights . . ." (T. S. Eliot, *The Complete Poems and Plays 1909–1950* [N.Y.: Harcourt, Brace, 1952], p. 42).

190.

Coney Island is a great fair attended on Sundays in the summer by more than a million people. They drink, shout, eat, wallow, and leave the ocean strewn with newspapers and the streets covered with tin cans, cigarette butts, bites of food, and shoes with broken heels. On its way home from the fair, the crowd sings and vomits in groups of a hundred over the railings of the boardwalk. In groups of a thousand it urinates in the corners, on abandoned boats, or on the monument to Garibaldi or to the unknown soldier.

You cannot imagine the loneliness a Spaniard feels there, especially an Andalusian. If you fall they will trample you, and if you slip into the water they will bury you under their lunch wrappers.

The rumble of that terrible multitude fills the whole Sunday of New York, pounding the hollow pavements with the rhythm of a stampede. [He reads "Landscape of a Vomiting Multitude."]

The solitude of the poems I wrote about the crowd rhymes with others of the same style, which I have no time to read, for instance the "Brooklyn Bridge Nocturne" and "Nightfall at Battery Place," where sailors and cheap women, soldiers and policemen dance on the tired sea, a pasture for siren cows, a promenade for bells and bellowing buoys.

The month of August is here. New York is leveled by heat, in the style of Écija,[12] and I must leave for the country.[13]

Green lake, landscape of hemlocks. Suddenly, in the

[12] A proverbially hot town ("The Frying Pan of Andalusia") in the province of Seville.
[13] In the following paragraph Lorca "conflates" two different summer trips: his visit to Ángel and Amelia del Río in Bushnellsville, New York, and his stay with Philip Cummings in Eden Mills, Vermont.

forest, a lost distaff. A little girl, Mary, who eats maple
syrup, and a little boy, Stanton, who plays the jew's-harp,
keep me company and patiently teach me the list of Amer-
ican Presidents. When we get to the great Lincoln, they
give him a military salute. Stanton's father owns four blind
horses that he bought in the village of Eden Mills.[14] The
mother almost always has a fever. I run, I drink good
water, and my mood sweetens among the hemlock trees
and my little friends. They introduce me to the Tyler girls,
penniless descendants of an old President, who live in a
cabin, take photographs which they title "Exquisite Si-
lence,"[15] and play, on an incredible spinet, songs from the
heroic age of Washington. They are old and very tiny and
they wear trousers so that the brambles won't scratch them,
but they have beautiful white hair and they hold hands and
listen to me improvise some songs just for them at the
spinet. Sometimes they invite me to dinner and give me
nothing but tea and a few pieces of cheese, but they assure
me that the teapot is genuine china and that there is jasmine
in the tea.[16] At the end of August they take me to their
cabin and say, "Haven't you noticed? Autumn is almost

[14] *One* blind horse, according to Stanton Hogan (Eisenberg, "Cuatro pes-
quisas," p. 12).

[15] A snapshot of a winter scene, entitled "Exquisite Silence," does indeed form
part of an album in the Lorca archive, presented to the poet by the Tyler sisters.

[16] Philip Cummings (Federico's host in Eden Mills, Vermont) writes: "The
two Miss Tylers [Elizabeth and Dorothea], who were splendid women, de-
pressed school teachers who had ended their careers and were planning to rebuild
a derelict farm, may or may not (I suspect not . . .) have been President Tyler's
relatives in a diluted way. Both are dead and they lost the farm because it could
not be saved by their pitiful efforts . . . In front of their property they rebuilt
with great effort the old stone wall which they called the Chinese Wall. Federico
and I added many a stone to it and heaved others into line. Then we would sit
on the wobbly porch and drink pots of tea and Federico said, 'Vamos a probar
otra desesperación de té' [Now we'll have another 'desperation' of tea']" (Letter
to C. Maurer, Nov. 12, 1985). See also Cummings's diary, "August in Eden,"
in García Lorca, *Songs*, tr. Philip Cummings, ed. Daniel Eisenberg (Pittsburgh:
Duquesne University Press, 1976), pp. 125–66.

192.

here." Sure enough, on the tables and spinet and all around the portrait of Tyler were the yellowest, reddest, most orange maple and grape leaves I had ever seen.

In such surroundings, of course, my poetry took on the tone of the forest. Tired of New York and yearning for the least significant, poorest living things, I wrote an insectary, which I cannot read to you in full, but where I begin by asking help from the Virgin, the Ave Maria Stella of those delightful Catholic folk. I wanted to sing to the insects who spend their lives flying and praising Our Lord with their little instruments.

The Poet Prays to the Virgin for Help[17]

I pray to the Divine Mother of God,
Heavenly Queen of all living things,
that she grant me the pure light of the little animals
that have a single letter in their vocabulary.
Animals without souls. Simple shapes.
Far from the cat's despicable knowledge.
Far from the owls' fictitious profundity.
Far from the horse's sculptural wisdom.
Creatures that love without eyes,
with a single sense of infinity's waves,
and that gather in great piles
to be eaten by the birds.
Grant me the single dimension
that little flat animals have
so that I can tell of things covered with earth
beneath the hard innocence of the shoe.
No one weeps because he understands

[17] This poem is erroneously titled "Luna y panorama de los insectos" in all previous studies and editions of Lorca. The source of the error is that the rough draft of the poem in the Lorca archives was begun on a sheet of paper previously used for "Luna y panorama de los insectos (poema de amor)."

193.

the millions of tiny deaths at the marketplace,
the Chinese multitude of headless onions,
and that great yellow sun of old, flattened fish.
You, Mother, forever to be feared. Whale of all the skies,
You Mother, forever joking. Neighbor of the borrowed
*   parsley.*
You know that to speak of the world,
I must understand its slightest flesh.[18]

But one day little Mary fell into a well and drowned. It would not be right to tell you of the deep sorrow, the true despair I felt that day. I will leave that to the trees and the walls that saw me.[19] At once I thought of that other little girl, from Granada,[20] whom I saw taken out of a cistern, her little hands entwined in the gaffs, her head knocking against the side, and the two girls, Mary and the other

---

[18] The text found in Eutimio Martín, pp. 191–93, is translated here by Simon and White. Rafael Martínez Nadal has published a fragment of the Virgin's reply in *El público* (Mexico: Joaquín Mortiz, 1974), pp. 193–94. Simon and White translate as follows: "The Holy Virgin Replies: But I pluck out my eyes of the giraffe. / And I replace them with the crocodile's eyes. / Because I am the Virgin Mary. / The flies see a black cloud of pepper. / But they are not the Virgin Mary. / I watch the crimes of the leaves, / the stinging pride of the wasps, / the indifferent mule driven crazy by the double moon / and the stable where the planet eats all its tiny offspring. / Because I am the Virgin Mary. // Solitude lives stuck in the mud . . ." A more complete manuscript of the poem was apparently given by Lorca to the French Hispanist Mathilde Pomès, but has since been lost. See Eutimio Martín, p. 191.

[19] The poet is speaking tongue in cheek. According to Ángel del Río, the death of Mary was a product of his "inventive fancy." See del Río, "Fotos de F.G.L. en Norteamérica (1929)," *Papeles de Son Armadans* XLII, no. cxxiv, p. 101; and Eisenberg, "Cuatro pesquisas," pp. 11–12.

[20] Lorca may be thinking of the imaginary drowned child mentioned in two poems of his *Diván del Tamarit* (1931–35). See "Ghazal V: The Dead Boy" and "First Casida: The Boy Wounded by the Water" (Spanish text in Mario Hernández, ed., *Diván del Tamarit, Llanto por Ignacio Sánchez Mejías, Sonetos* [Madrid: Alianza Editorial, 1981], pp. 67, 79–80). The theme recurs in the "Noiturnio do adoescente morto" in *Seis poemas galegos*. See M. Hernández, ed., *Primeras canciones, Seis poemas galegos, Poemas sueltos, Colección de canciones populares antiguas* (Madrid: Alianza, 1981), pp. 88–89.

one, became the same child, who cried and cried, unable to leave the circle of the well, in the unmoving water that never reaches the sea. ["Little Girl Drowned in the Well (Granada and Newburgh)."]

With the little girl dead, I could stay in the house no longer. Stanton was sadly eating the syrup his sister had left him, and the divine Miss Tylers were madly taking pictures of the autumn woods to give me as presents.

I went down to the lake, and the silent water, the cuckoo, etc., etc., made it impossible for me to sit. Every way that I stood or sat made me feel like a Romantic lithograph below which was written, "Federico lets his thoughts wander."[21] But at last a splendid line of Garcilaso put an end to that statuesque obsession. The line of Garcilaso:

Nuestro ganado pace, el viento espira
Our flocks graze, the wind sends forth its breath[22]

And this "Double Poem of Lake Eden Mills" was born. [He reads.]

Summer vacation is over, for "Saturn stops the trains," and I have to get back to New York. The drowned girl, Stanton the Little Sugar-Eater, and the trouser-wearing sisters stay with me for a long time. The train races along the Canadian frontier, and I feel unhappy and miss my little friends. The girl withdraws into the well, in a host of green angels, and on the boy's chest the cruel star of

[21] Lorca describes his state of mind in a lovely letter to Ángel del Río from Eden Mills: "It never stops raining. This family is very nice, full of gentle charm, but the woods and lake immerse me in a hardly bearable state of poetic desperation. I write all day and at night I feel drained . . . Now night is falling. The oil lamps have been lit and my whole childhood comes back to me, wrapped in a glory of poppies and grainfields. Among the ferns I've found a distaff covered with spiders and in the lake not one frog sings" (*Selected Letters*, tr. David Gershator [N.Y.: New Directions, 1983], p. 150).

[22] Garcilaso, Eclogue II, verse 1146.

195.

the North American police begins to grow, like saltpeter on a damp wall.

And then once again the frenzied rhythm of New York. But it no longer surprises me. I know the mechanism of the streets and talk to people and penetrate a bit deeper into social life. And I denounce it. For I have come from the countryside and do not believe that man is the most important thing in the world. ["New York (Office and Denunciation)."][23]

Time is passing, and this is not the time to read more poems. We have to leave New York. I won't read the poems about Christmas or the poems about the port.[24] Someday you will read them in the book, if you are interested.

Time is passing, and I am already on the ship taking me away from the howling city toward the beautiful Antilles. My first impression, that that world has no roots, stays with me . . .

Because if the wheel forgets its formula,
it will sing naked with herds of horses;
and if a flame burns the frozen blueprints,
the sky will have to flee before the tumult of windows.[25]

Edges and rhythm, form and anguish, the sky is swallowing them all. No longer does tower battle cloud, no longer do swarms of windows devour more than half the night. Flying fish weave moist garlands, and the sky, like that terrible big blue woman of Picasso, rushes over the sea with open arms.

[23] The title is not given in the manuscript, but Lorca leaves half a page blank, and the pagination jumps from 35 to 38.

[24] It is unclear which poems Lorca is referring to; Martín (p. 77) believes he means "Cementerio judío," but the maritime imagery in that composition hardly makes it a "poem about the port."

[25] From "Dance of Death."

The sky has conquered the skyscrapers, and from a distance New York's architecture seems prodigious and, no matter what was intended, moves one as much as a sight of nature, a mountain, or a desert. The Chrysler Building defends itself from the sun with its huge silver beak, and bridges, ships, railways, and men seem deafened and chained: chained by a cruel economic system whose throat must soon be cut, and deafened by excessive discipline and because they lack a sufficient dose of madness.

At any rate, I was leaving New York with a certain sadness and with profound admiration. I was leaving many friends there, and it had given me the most useful experience of my life. I must thank it for many things, especially for the holograph blues and the British stamp greens given me by the New Jersey shoreline as I strolled with Anita the Portuguese Indian and Sofía Megwinoff the Russian Puerto Rican, and for that divine aquarium and that zoo[26] where I felt like a child and remembered all the children in the world.

But the ship is getting farther away, and we are beginning to come to palm trees and cinnamon, the perfume of the America with roots, God's America, Spanish America.[27]

But what is this? Is it Spain again? Universal Andalusia? It is the yellow of Cádiz, but a shade brighter; the rosiness of Seville, but more like carmine; the green of Granada, but slightly phosphorescent like a fish.

Havana rises up amid cane fields and the noise of maracas, cornets, bells and marimbas. And who should come

[26] The Bronx Zoo, with which Lorca was much impressed.

[27] Lorca seems to be remembering the Nicaraguan poet Rubén Darío, whose ode "To Roosevelt" celebrates "la América católica, la América española." The poem ends on these words: "Y, pues contáis con todo, falta una cosa: ¡Dios!" ("And, as you have everything, only one thing is missing: God!").

197.

to welcome me at the port but the dark Trinidad of my childhood, who used to stroll "along the pier of Havana."[28]

And the blacks are there, with rhythms I discover are typical of the great Andalusian people—blacks without tragedy who roll their eyes and say, "We are Latins."

Against three great horizontal lines—the line of the cane fields, that of the terraces, and that of the palm trees—a thousand blacks, their cheeks dyed orange, as though running a fever of 150 degrees, dance this *son*[29] which I composed and which comes to us like a breeze from the island: ["Blacks Dancing to Cuban Rhythms"].

[28] From a Spanish popular song: "Por el muelle de la Habana, / paseaba una mañana / la morena Trinidad" ("Along the pier of Havana one morning, dark Trinidad was strolling").

[29] An Afro-Cuban dance in syncopated rhythm which originated in Santiago de Cuba (Oriente province) toward the end of the eighteenth century. Lorca borrowed his refrain from a popular *son*. His friend the poet Nicolás Guillén (*b.* 1905) published eight poems inspired by the *son* [*Motivos de son*] in Havana in April 1930. It was Guillén who had delighted Lorca with the words "We are Latins . . ."

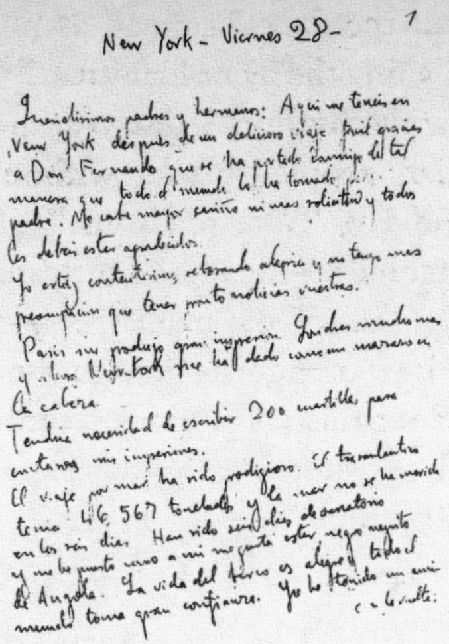

New York - Viernes 28 -

[handwritten letter in Spanish]

THE POET

WRITES TO

HIS FAMILY

FROM NEW YORK

AND HAVANA

Translated by Christopher Maurer

[Lorca's first letter home from New York,
June 28, 1929]

New York, Friday the 28th [*of June 1929*]

Dearest family,

Well, here I am in New York, after a delightful voyage, an easy one thanks to Don Fernando,[1] who was so kind to me that everyone took him for my father. One cannot imagine a more affectionate, solicitous person, and you should all feel grateful to him.

I feel content, full of joy, and my one worry is getting news from you soon.

Paris impressed me very much, London even more, and now New York has given me the knock-out punch.

I would have to write two hundred pages to give you all my impressions.

The sea voyage was marvelous.[2] The liner was 46,567 tons, and the ocean was completely calm for all six days. They were like six days of convalescence and I have gotten a real tan: as black as blackest Africa. Life on board a ship is quite gay, and people confide in each other right away. I had a little five-year-old friend, a lovely boy from Hungary who was going to America to meet his father for the first time (the father had left before he was born). He played with me, and we grew so close that he broke into tears when we said goodbye, and, needless to say, so did I. This is the subject of my first poem, this child whom I will never see again, this rose of Hungary who disappears into the belly of New York, seeking his fortune; life will be cruel or kind to him, and I will be but a remote memory,

---

[1] Fernando de los Ríos Urruti (1879–1949), who had been one of García Lorca's professors in the Faculty of Law of the University of Granada, later Minister of Education in the Second Republic, and a leading member of the Socialist Party, was on his way to Columbia University and Puerto Rico to give a series of lectures on sixteenth-century political thought.

[2] García Lorca had arrived three days earlier on the White Star liner *Olympic*, sister ship of the *Titanic* (Daniel Eisenberg, "A Chronology of Lorca's Visit to New York and Cuba," *Kentucky Romance Quarterly* XXIV [1977], p. 235).

201.

connected with the rhythm of the huge ship and the ocean.[3]

On arriving in New York, one feels overwhelmed, but not frightened. I found it uplifting to see how man can use science and technology to make something as impressive as a spectacle of nature. It is incredible. The port and the lights of the skyscrapers, easily confused with the stars, the millions of other lights, and the rivers of automobiles are a sight like no other on earth. Paris and London are two tiny villages compared with this vibrant, maddening Babel.

When the ship pulled in, I had a great surprise. A group of Spaniards was there waiting for us: Ángel del Río,[4] the professor Federico Onís, the poet León Felipe, a handful of journalists, the managing editor of *La Prensa*,[5] and . . . brace yourselves! . . . MAROTO!! Maroto, who went crazy hugging and even kissing me.[6] He has just arrived from Mexico, and is earning a lot of money as a painter and commercial artist.

They have been extremely good to me, as has the entire Spanish colony. I can now see what a good thing it is to have become a bit famous: all doors are opened, and everyone treats you with distinction.

Both Federico Onís and his wife have shown me great affection. They are admirers of mine, two *lorquistas* (as they say).

Onís is a professor at Columbia, and it was he who arranged what pleases me most: I am now a student at

[3] No such poem has ever been found.

[4] Ángel del Río (1901–62), an excellent literary critic and historian, was then an instructor in Columbia's Department of Spanish and Portuguese, directed by Federico de Onís Sánchez (1885–1966), disciple of Miguel de Unamuno, who had emigrated to New York in 1916.

[5] José Camprubí, father-in-law of the Spanish poet Juan Ramón Jiménez.

[6] Gabriel García Maroto (*b.* 1889), Spanish painter and illustrator, who had published Lorca's first book of poetry (*Libro de poemas*) eight years earlier.

Columbia University and I live in a dormitory here, surrounded by American students.

Federico Onís did not want me to live at the International House because, he said, everyone there is a foreigner, and there are so many South Americans that I would always be speaking Spanish. "We must surround the poet with English speakers," he said, "so that he will have to make an effort."

It is difficult to become a student at the university of New York [sic], but because Don Fernando teaches here and Onís is one of its most renowned professors, they have managed to get me in.

The university is marvelous. It is located on the bank of the Hudson River, in the heart of the city, on the island of Manhattan, the best part, and is very close to the great avenues. And yet it is delightfully quiet. My room is on the ninth floor,[7] and it overlooks the playing fields, with their green grass and statues.

To one side, below the windows of the rooms just across the hall, is Broadway, the immense boulevard which runs from one end of New York to the other.

It would be foolish to even try to describe the immensity of the skyscrapers and the traffic. Everything I could say would fall short. All Granada would fit into three of these buildings. Just one of these little "houses" could hold thirty thousand people or so.

I will write and give you my impressions.

But meanwhile you should know that my room is very inexpensive and very lovely, with a splendid view; that I am enrolled in an English language and literature class; and that I feel like working. Know also that I will never be able to thank you for all you have done for me, but that

[7] Lorca actually occupied room 617, Furnald Hall.

I will repay you with a work and a way of life that will make you proud and happy. But no doubt I am lucky with people. I feel as though I had been here all my life, and I haven't had any problems whatsoever in this sprawling Babel.

In fact, once you get over your first impressions and first sense of fright, it is very easy to get around New York: much easier than Paris and infinitely easier than London, for all the streets are numbered, and the entire city is mathematically laid out in blocks, the only way to organize the chaos and motion. In a word, I feel well adjusted. New York is an extremely gay, friendly place. The people are naïve and charming. I feel good here, better than in Paris, which I found a bit old and a bit rotten.

But, as I started to say, what happens to *me* is always unusual.

Last night I went to the heart of immense Broadway with León Felipe, Maroto, and a certain Mr. Flores, who is the editor of an English-language magazine that deals with Spanish things.[8] Broadway at night was breathtaking: the towering skyscrapers are covered with brightly colored illuminated signs that blink and change with the most unheard-of, marvelous rhythms. Streams of blues and greens and yellows and reds changing and leaping into the sky, higher than the moon, blinking on and off with the names of banks and hotels and automobiles and film companies.

[8]Ángel Flores (*b.* 1900), literary critic, editor of numerous anthologies of Spanish literature and of the short-lived magazine *Alhambra*, and translator of T. S. Eliot's *The Waste Land* (*Tierra baldía* [Barcelona: Editorial Cervantes, 1930]), a book which Lorca probably saw in manuscript in New York. Flores was also director of the Hispano and American Alliance (Forty-second Street and Fifth Avenue), where Lorca spent some of his free time. It was he who introduced Lorca to the American poet Hart Crane. See B. Bussell Thompson and J. K. Walsh, "Un encuentro de Lorca y Hart Crane en Nueva York," *Insula* XLI, no. 479 (Oct. 1986), p. 1.

The motley crowd of bright sweaters and bold scarves rising and falling in five or six different streams, the horns of the cars together with the shouting and the music from the radios, and brightly lit airplanes passing overhead with ads for hats, clothes, and toothpaste, changing their letters and playing great trumpets and bells. It is a magnificent, moving spectacle put on by the boldest, most modern city in the world.

Suddenly, when I was most absorbed and enthralled by all this, I hear a loud voice from the window of a large restaurant, calling "Federrico! Federrico!" and I see a boy in a red silk shirt leap out the window to the street, almost breaking his leg, and he comes up and hugs me. It was the Englishman Colin Hackforth, who visited me in Granada and became a close friend.[9] I felt very happy, for you can imagine how difficult and how unheard-of it is for two people to meet like this in New York. It is as unusual as two fishes meeting in the middle of the ocean.

Maroto was astonished. "The same as ever. This could only happen to you." I was truly lucky, for Colin is a writer, a very good one, and he will be the best possible English teacher. He is going to come to the university and we will translate things together every day at six, after I finish my work, and he his. In fact, last night he was already pointing things out to me in English, and he taught me a great number of words. Between him and Onís, who will introduce me to some American girls, I will be forced to make some progress with my English, and Colin is also going to try to find me a French person to converse with.

[9] Campbell Hackforth-Jones (b. 1905) met García Lorca in Granada during the Christmas holidays of 1926–27. Having graduated from Oxford, he was serving an apprenticeship in a brokerage firm on Wall Street. See Andrew A. Anderson, "Una amistad inglesa de García Lorca," Ínsula XL, no. 462 (May 1985), pp. 3–4.

Here's another strange thing. Do you remember my telling you about a young American poet who wrote a poem to me in the Residencia after hearing me play the piano?[10] I met him again on the train from Madrid to Paris, and he invited me to spend the month of August (the hottest month here) in his house in Canada. His father is a railroad broker, and he will send me the tickets free. Don Fernando told me not to miss this opportunity to visit one of the most beautiful places in North America; to get there, one passes by Niagara Falls. He is a fine boy; he has studied at Columbia and Onís knows him. Last year, as an exercise in his Spanish class, he translated two of the *Gypsy Ballads* into English. In other words, he knows me and hasn't invited me for just any old reason. I've accepted and, God willing, if all goes as planned, I'll spend the month of August in Canada.

American customs are nothing like Spanish ones. Here they invite you places at the drop of a hat.

Before I forget, here is my address:

> Mister Federico G. Lorca (like that)
> Furnald Hall
> Columbia University
> New York City
> E.S.A. [*sic*]

I hope you will write me often. I will do so, too, and (as you can see from this one) I'll write you long letters.

---

[10] Philip H. Cummings (*b.* 1906), a writer whom García Lorca had met at the Residencia de Estudiantes, Madrid, in July 1928. Cummings remembers the train ride from Madrid to Paris: "We stretched out and he [Lorca] talked for hours to the rhythmic click of the wheels over the rails, of what life was for and that man was always playing hide and seek with death . . . 'Felipe, life is laughter, amid a rosary of deaths; it is to look beyond the braying man to the love in the heart of the people. It is being the wind and ruffling the waters of a brook. It is coming from nowhere and going to nowhere and being everywhere with many tears around you.' " See García Lorca, *Songs*, pp. 178–79.

But my letters would have to be even longer for me to give you all my impressions and prove how often I remember you.

But the person I can't get out of my head is Paco. Please send me a cablegram as soon as you know the results of his exams.[11] And, needless to say, you shouldn't worry. For even if he fails, he will triumph next year.

Please don't forget this: it's important to me.

I feel perfectly fine, and there is plenty to eat. I am surrounded by friends, by people who take an interest in me. I have tried to be nice to them and, of course, have managed to do so.

Mother must go to Lanjarón,[12] and Father, too. It will be very good for him, and if you don't go, you'll both have an attack of trigeminal neuralgia.

I was greatly saddened by Franco's accident.[13] Such things are doubly sad from afar. He was a very brave man who came to an unfortunate end, but one full of greatness and heroism.

The weather is delightful today. It is beginning to rain, and a cool breeze is riffling the trees and the vaporous shirts of the boys playing tennis.

Lots of hugs and kisses.

You are probably in the Huerta[14] listening to the tinkling

[11] Federico's younger brother, Francisco (1902–76), was in Madrid studying for the qualifying exams for the Spanish diplomatic corps.

[12] A spa in the mountainous Alpujarras region of Granada which Lorca often visited with his family. "Strange Berber Andalusia," he calls it in a letter, "where one can understand the wounds of St. Roque, tears of blood, and the taste for the buried knife" (OC, Vol. III, p. 970).

[13] The Spanish aviator Ramón Franco Bahamonde (1856–1938), brother of Francisco Franco, was presumed dead after an accident during a transatlantic flight to New York. Two days after this letter was written, he was found alive, together with his crew.

[14] The Huerta de San Vicente, the Lorca family's summer house on the outskirts of Granada.

207.

bells from the Seminary and the distant bells of the Cathedral. I am listening to the sirens and the murmur of New York.

Give my best to the whole family, and don't forget anyone: Aunt Isabel, Aunt Matilde, Clotilde,[15] Mama-yaya, the girls, and all our friends. All my love.

Federico

Write soon!
Farewell.

June 6 [sic for July 6, 1929]—New York

Dear family:

You have probably already received my first letter, in which I gave you my impressions of New York and my address in this huge city.

I didn't want Father's birthday to slip by without sending him a big hug and warmest birthday greetings.

I have already begun my English classes at the university. I take them in the same building I live in,[1] and the dining hall is also there, so I do everything without any need to go outside and work up a sweat. My room is lovely, and there is always a breeze. It's the highest point in the city, alongside the river, and it is quite cool.

I still haven't felt the heat. It is exactly the same temperature here as it is in Granada, and my room and the whole campus are as cool as a garden. What is truly dread-

---

[15]Matilde and Isabel García Rodríguez, paternal aunts, and Clotilde García Picossi, the poet's cousin. It is uncertain whom Lorca means by Mama-yaya.

[1] Lorca had enrolled in "English for Beginners," taught by Amy I. Shaw and given in room 503, Journalism Building, "a course for educated foreigners who have practically no knowledge of spoken English" (Eisenberg, "Cuatro pesquisas," p. 1).

ful in summer is to go downtown and mingle with the throngs of autos and people, but you have to admit that it is equally dreadful to cross the Embovedado on a July afternoon. Night at Columbia is delightful, here beside the river, and in fact everywhere else in the city.

I think I have a certain talent for English. We'll see!

My friends here continue to be extraordinarily kind to me, and I haven't had a single bad moment. The poet León Felipe, a professor at Cornell University, and his wife[2] have been like parents, and have been keeping me safe and sound. Yesterday I had a visit from the son of the Duke of Tovar, who is studying at Columbia, and who offered to do whatever he could for me. A very nice boy, a believer in democracy, and a great admirer of the United States.[3] I went to a party for some Mexican painters and poets— people I knew of but had never met—and guess who else was there? Miss Adams, the girl I saw so much of in Granada.[4] It's a small, small world! Speaking of strange coincidences, in England I ran into the girl who was staying at Don Fernando's house. She asked me to remember her to you.[5]

These first few days I have been getting to know New York. Last Sunday I went to Coney Island, an island at the mouth of the Hudson, an amusement park with arcades and all sorts of extraordinary things. Like everything else

[2] Berta Gamboa (d. 1957).

[3] Don Rafael de Figueroa y Bermejillo, son of Rodrigo de Figueroa y Torres, third Duke of Tovar, lived in Lorca's dormitory (John Jay Hall) during the fall term, 1929–30.

[4] Mildred Adams Kenyon (1894–1979), journalist, translator of Ortega y Gasset, and later author of *García Lorca: Playwright and Poet* (N.Y.: Braziller, 1977), had met Lorca in Granada in April 1928.

[5] The British Hispanist Helen Grant, who was then studying Spanish and French at Oxford. Gibson, p. 610.

here, it is monstrously huge. According to the newspapers, there were more than a million visitors that day.[6] I can't even begin to describe the color and movement on the beach, with throngs of twenty and thirty thousand people. The amusement park is truly a child's dream. There are incredible roller coasters, tunnels of love, music, freak shows, dance halls, wild animals, Ferris wheels and all sorts of rides, the world's fattest women,[7] a four-eyed man, etc. etc., and thousands of stalls selling a fantastic variety of ice cream, hot dogs, French fries, little buns, and candies. The crowd rolls through the island with the sweaty, salty murmur of the sea: a crowd of Jews, blacks, Japanese, Chinese, mulattoes, and blond-haired Yankees.

It is an amazing sight, but it is simply *too much*, and one visit is enough. The people drawn to this island of games are the real *people* of New York, the salt of the earth. One hardly ever sees an automobile: you get there on the subway and on paddle boats, which is how I myself arrived, floating down the river under a lovely blue Sevillian sky.

When night came, all the lights were lit, and it was like a childhood dream—the big golden Ferris wheels, the brilliant towers of wood and glass, with the music and the sound of the rides in the background.

My friends did their best to get me to speak English, and made me ask for things. You wouldn't believe what

[6] Lorca probably visited Coney Island not on a Sunday but on the Fourth of July, 1929: according to the next day's *New York Times*, there were over a million persons there.

[7] Among them Etta, whom the *Times* describes as "400 pounds of pulchritude," corollary of "the fat lady" who appears in Lorca's "Landscape of a Vomiting Multitude." In 1929, Coney Island, which was turning "from a tinsel town to a substantial suburb of a great city," complained of "a growing scarcity of dog-faced men, mermaids and many legged livestock . . . On the entire Island this Summer there are only three pairs of Siamese twins and but two editions of the strongest man in the world" ("Coney Enters Its Steel Age," *The New York Times*, June 16, 1929, IX, p. 2).

I went through, but I did very well, to everyone's great amusement.

I haven't yet gotten a letter from you, and you can imagine how I would love to receive one. I hope you will all write me, and that your letters will be long and unhurried, and that the girls will write, too, so I will get news of everyone. As you can see, I'm writing you at greater length than I ever have, and I will continue to do so, so that each seven or eight days you will have news from me.

To give you some idea of the size of Columbia University, let me say that close to 16,000 students have enrolled in the summer session, which lasts until August 18.[8] This place is like a fairgrounds. The girls are extremely pretty, a little wild in the way they dress, but full of charm and personality. I'm going to practice my English with one of them, but I want to make sure I get the prettiest, and not commit myself without seeing her first. It would be terrible to end up with some chatterbox who wouldn't teach me anything, and then—well, what a nuisance to get rid of her! But seriously, this is the only way to learn English. Having a conversation partner is useful, for that way one can avoid pure grammar and learn the colloquial expressions for things.

I hope you haven't forgotten my address:

> Mister Federico G. Lorca
> Furnald Hall
> Columbia University
> New York City
> E.S.A. [sic]

[8] Almost 14,000 students had enrolled in the summer session. Among them were five hundred foreigners, mostly from China, Japan, Mexico, and Cuba. During the 1929–30 academic year, Columbia had the largest student population in the country (*The New York Times*, June 9, 1929, p. 28, and *Columbia Spectator*, Dec. 16, 1929, p. 3).

No harm in repeating it, just in case you forgot or my letter was lost.

I long for news from Paquito. I wrote him at the Residencia de Estudiantes and he must have received my letter by now.

You can't imagine how I miss you all, and I hope you are well. I'm fine, in fact I am rather happy. Would you send me your photos—of Father, Mother, and the girls—to put in my room?

I will send you the latest issue of the *Revista de Estudios Hispánicos*, New York, which has just published an article on my poetry.[9]

On Monday there is a meeting of the Spanish students to plan the Spanish party they will give at the end of the semester. I am in charge of the chorus.[10] I'm going to make these Americans sing the *cachucha* "Por la calle abajito," and some *sevillanas*. It will be hilarious to hear them say *carrrra* instead of *cara*.

Would you believe there are over six hundred students of Spanish language and literature? Take care. I will write again in a few days. But write me soon. Hugs and kisses and much love from your son and brother,

Federico

Sunday, 14 [July 1929], New York

Dear family,

My life in New York goes peacefully on. I'm very good at adapting to new circumstances, and I feel fine in this

[9] An intelligent review of *Primer romancero gitano* by León Felipe had appeared in *Revista de Estudios Hispánicos* II (April–June 1929), pp. 193–97.

[10] "Hardly had he arrived in New York, when he adopted a title, and one moreover neither short nor humble: 'Director of the Mixed Choruses of the Instituto de las Españas in the United States of America' " (Daniel Solana, "Federico García Lorca," *Alhambra* [N.Y.] I, no. 3 [Aug. 1929], p. 24).

new environment, which is so different, but, to me, very suggestive.

On Isabelita's saint's day, I sent her a cable using the Acera del Casino address, and the cable was returned to me: "Addressee Unknown." I was furious, for I imagined that Señor Raigón's maids had simply said, "She doesn't live here," and refused to accept the cable. I didn't want to try again, because the cable cost two dollars to send, but this oughtn't to happen again, and you should tell them to accept all the mail that is sent there. It seems very, very sad that Isabelita is an "unknown addressee" at Acera del Casino, 31, Granada.

The telegraph company is a very reliable one. Someone over *there* is to blame. I was extremely angry, for I wanted you to get news from me, and wanted to wish Isabelita a happy saint's day. The important thing is that it not happen again.

My English class at the university is great fun. It includes Japanese, Chinese, blacks, Indians, a heavily made-up sixty-year-old Cuban lady named Ofelia, and me. The teacher speaks only English, and she is excellent.

I have to lug the dictionary around with me all day, for these Americans are very nice and are always asking me questions and trying to strike up a conversation. In my residence hall there is a Jewish boy, of Russian origin, who has been talking my ears off. He is greatly interested in Spain and is always asking me questions. Naturally, each question and answer require fifteen minutes of word hunting in the dictionary. But it is the only way to learn.

Yesterday I had tea with Miss Adams, and she has invited me to spend next Sunday at her house in the country. The Sunday after that (from Saturday morning on), I am going to Onís's farm, on the banks of the Hudson, three hours from New York, and the Sunday after that (you can see how little free time I have), I'm going to make a trip to the country with two girls who are friends and "old admirers" of mine: two lovely girls from Puerto Rico, home of the most beautiful women in America.

I have also met a famous black writer, Nella Larsen, of the literary avant-garde, and with her I visited the black neighborhood and saw much that surprised me. To my great amazement, everyone understands my French. With this writer I spoke French the whole afternoon, and we managed to say whatever we felt like. Necessity, mother of invention, worked a miracle or two! The little French that I knew came back to me, and I remembered all the words. And that made me very happy indeed.

This writer is an exquisitely kind woman, full of the deep, moving melancholy that all blacks have. She gave a party at her house, and there were only blacks. This is the second time I've gone somewhere with her, for she interests me enormously.

At the last party, I was the only white. She lives on Second Avenue, and from her windows you could see all the lights of New York. It was night and beacons were sweeping back and forth across the sky. The blacks sang and danced.

What marvelous songs! Only the *cante jondo*[1] is comparable to them.

There was a little boy who sang religious songs. I sat down at the piano, and I sang, too. And you wouldn't believe how much they liked my songs. They made me sing some of them four or five times: the "Moricas de Jaén," "No salgas, paloma, al campo," and "El burro."

---

[1] Generic term for a type of Andalusian song, dance, and guitar music also known as flamenco. See Lorca's essay "Deep Song," in C. Maurer, tr., *Deep Song and Other Prose*, pp. 23–41.

The blacks are an extremely kind people. When I said goodbye, they all hugged me, and the writer gave me her books, with warm dedications—they told me this was quite an honor, for she has never done that for any of them.

At the party there was a black woman who was, without exaggeration, the loveliest, most beautiful woman I have ever seen in all my life. It would be impossible to imagine more perfect features, or a more perfect body. She danced a sort of rumba, accompanied by a tom-tom (African drum), and her dance was a sight as pure and as tender as the moon over the sea, or some such simple and eternal thing in Nature. You can imagine how delighted I was by that party. With the same writer, I was in an all-black cabaret, and I kept thinking of Mother: it was one of those places you sometimes see in the movies, and which terrify her.

The most interesting thing about this city is this very mixture of different races and customs. I hope to study them all, and make some sense of this chaos and complexity.

I have also attended the church services of several different religions, and have come out of them with a fresh enthusiasm for our prodigiously beautiful, unequaled Spanish Catholicism. I will say nothing of the Protestant cults, for I simply can't get it into my head—my Latin head—how people can be Protestant. It's the most ridiculous, most odious thing in the world.

Imagine a church where, instead of a main altar, there is an organ, and, in front of the organ, a man in a frock (the pastor) who is speaking. Then everyone sings for a while, and out the door they go. They have suppressed all that is human and comforting and (in a word) beautiful. Even American Catholicism is different. It is undermined by Protestantism, and has the same coldness. This morning I attended a Catholic Mass, said by an Englishman. And

I now see how miraculously an Andalusian priest says the Mass. The Spanish people have an innate sense of beauty and a lofty sense of God's presence in the temple. I can now understand the uniqueness of the Spanish Mass, the most fervent of all spectacles. The slowness, the grandeur, the adornment of the altar, the cordiality and fellow feeling in the adoration of the Blessed Sacrament, the cult of the Virgin . . . in Spain all this has a personality of its own, with an enormous poetry and beauty.

I also understand, here in New York, face to face with the Protestant churches, the racial reasons for Spain's great struggle against Protestantism, and the truly Spanish attitude of Philip II, a great king whom history has treated unjustly.

What American Catholicism lacks is solemnity; i.e., human warmth. When it comes to religion, solemnity means cordiality, for it is living proof (proof for the senses) of the immediate presence of God. As though to say, "God is with us. Let us render him homage and glory." It is a great mistake to suppress the element of pure ceremony. That is one of the great things about Spain, these exquisite forms, this sense of nobility in the way God is treated.

And yet . . . as I watched the Catholic parishioners this morning, I saw signs of extraordinary devotion, above all among the men, a rare thing in Spain. Many took Communion, and it was a serious, extraordinarily disciplined group, with no nonsense.

I saw some Japanese children make their First Communion—their little yellow faces, their white clothing, the most delicate, tender thing you can imagine.

The religious problem is important to see and to study in the United States.

I have also been to a Jewish synagogue, the one for

Spanish Jews.[2] I heard some extremely beautiful chants, and the cantor was a true prodigy of voice and emotion. But I realize that in Granada almost all of us are Jews. It was amazing—they all looked as if they had been born in Granada. There were more than twenty of them, who ran the gamut from Don Manuel López Saez to Miguel Carmona. The rabbi is named Sola,[3] and has the same pallid complexion as Solá Segura, who is probably his relative. I was doing my best not to laugh. There was a very solemn, beautiful ceremony, but I found it meaningless. To me the figure of Christ seems too strong to deny.

What was truly extraordinary was the chanting. The chants were extraordinary, heartrending, disconsolate. It was a continuous, long, and strikingly beautiful lament.

Some other time I will tell you about other things I've seen. I don't see much of the Spaniards. I prefer to live the life of an American. It isn't hot at all. Two hot days are always followed by two cool ones. Today it is delightful. Much cooler than in Granada. But remember, I live by the side of the river, in the highest spot in the city. I imagine you have already received my letters. Once I get settled, I am going to write you twice a week. You do the same, and give me all sorts of news, and get the girls to write, and mail your letters immediately, so they'll get here soon.

I am feeling fine. The food is good, and I lead a calm, quiet sort of existence. This high and lofty room, full of silence (relative silence), doesn't really give one an idea of New York.

[2] Shearith Israel, at Central Park West and Seventieth Street. The congregation's burial ground (Oliver Street and New Bowery) is the "cementerio judío" of Lorca's poem.

[3] David de Sola Pool (1885–1970), an authority on the Sephardic Jews and on the history of Shearith Israel.

217.

Best to everyone. For you, hugs and kisses from your son (and brother)

Tell Paco to write.

[c. *July 24, 1929*]

Dear family,

I have gotten two letters from Mother and a letter from the girls. You can't imagine how happy I am to know you are all well. I'm very sorry you are feeling bored, but I, too, grow bored when I am all alone in my room around noon when I settle down to work and there is no family silliness and no "illuminated coffee."[1] Write me nice long letters, and tell me all that is happening. That is what *I'm* doing, isn't it? I will always be delighted and amused to hear from you. I want you to have all my news, and not worry about me. But you must write back to me.

The photos of the girls came out very well, they're lovely. I've hung them in my room. But I also want photos of you. Take a picture of yourselves in the Huerta and send it to me. I keep remembering that Mother should go to Lanjarón, without fail.

You ought to help Paquito keep up his spirits, whether he passes or fails his exams. If he fails, it isn't his fault: he has worked hard, *very* hard, and on the next set of exams he will do splendidly. I know there isn't any need to tell you this, for you're a wonderful family, like no other in the world, but there's no harm in everyone putting in his own two cents. Anyway, if Paquito passes, I want you to send me a cable, *ipso facto*. They get here the same day. I got your cable on my birthday, and I suppose you received

[1] Family name for coffee laced with liqueur.

218.

mine. Since there is a six-hour time difference, you may have gotten mine a little late. But it only takes two or three hours.

I celebrated my birthday and, needless to say, thought of you often. I spent the whole day working, and at night some friends came to get me and we went to visit a certain editor and writer, an important Hispanist named Mr. Brickell.[2] There was a little party, and—I couldn't get out of it!—they made me play the piano and sing. You have no idea how these Americans love Spanish songs. I have a real following here! And since they tell all their friends, Mr. Brickell's house was packed. I have to admit, hardly anyone knows more songs than I. They were simply amazed. This winter, for sure, I am going to give a recital of Spanish popular music at some really fashionable salon.[3] This is great propaganda for Spain and, above all, for Andalusia. So . . . my birthday had a happy ending, although I couldn't have imagined that all of *you* were going to be ferreted away indoors. I thought you would be outside, in the cool, admirable wind of Granada.

Summer is behaving itself. We have had six very cool days—cool enough to wear a vest (imagine me in a vest!). Now it is starting to warm up a bit, and return to normal.

[2] Henry Herschel Brickell (1889–1952), book reviewer for *The New York Evening Post* and the *North American Review*, and an editor at Henry Holt and Company. For his memories of García Lorca, see "A Spanish Poet in New York," *Virginia Quarterly Review* XXI (1945), pp. 386–98.

[3] "Some of the parties given for him were not as successful. A woman's club . . . gave a dinner in his honor where he shared attention with a singer of American folk songs named Jack Niles. Folk music was supposed to be a bond between them. Both of them sang for their supper, both were applauded, neither understood the other's language. Had Federico sung in French, he would have been understood. As it was, the audience cheered for his charm; and as he departed the limp that always signaled fatigue showed in his walk" (Mildred Adams, pp. 125–26).

I get up early and study English, then I go to class next door. I eat here at the university, and go back to my room, get freshened up, and sit down to write, or go on with English. At seven o'clock, in broad daylight, I eat dinner and go out for a walk, or go to a party or meeting of some sort until eleven, and then to bed. There are more parties and gatherings here than anyplace else in the world. Americans cannot stand to be alone. I am always turning down invitations. They are getting to be a nuisance, and I have decided to go only to the ones I like, or the ones that seem useful, but no others. If they catch you off guard, the old women intellectuals here will devour you. The day before yesterday, late afternoon or early evening, I went to visit a Peruvian girl, an "admirer" of mine (God deliver us!). Actually, it wasn't as bad as I expected. She had invited me so that I could meet five or six incredibly beautiful South American girls. Some were blond, others dark, others brunette. This woman seems to have invited every shade imaginable, in order to delight her guest. No invitation could have been more exquisite. We chatted away and when dinnertime came (this was about a quarter to eight), she invited us to stay for dinner. I ought to explain that only very rich Americans have maids, and in that pretty little apartment there were none. So we had to cook for ourselves. I took off my jacket and put on an apron. One of the girls made me a paper chef's hat, and I washed the plates and spoons. Everyone worked. They made some sort of dish with corn on the cob and butter and chicken and rice, and later fruit and wonderful coffee, since the hostess has spent most of her life in Puerto Rico.

Then we set the table, and the table was beautiful: the glassware was blue, and amazingly delicate. There's de-

220.

mocracy for you: the table settings were lovely, but we had to set the table ourselves, for there is no serving class. Yesterday I carefully sewed on my first buttons. They're on so sturdily that if you tried to get them off you'd take a piece of the pants with them. I sewed them on much better than any of *you* ever did, not to mention Castilla, who sticks them on with spit!

I have spent some money, but not very much. The first few days, naturally, I wasn't sure where things were cheapest, and had to find out for myself, and ended up paying more. The American diet is very healthy. Mother could live happily here, for she has good taste and enjoys all sorts of food. But when I think of Father in one of these restaurants I die of laughter. I can imagine him trying to catch the first ship that would deposit him, six or seven days later, in Gibraltar or Vigo. Keep writing. I have written this today, and tomorrow, or the day after, I'll write again. And please write long letters. You can write to Don Fernando, % Don Federico Onís. Say hello to the whole family for me, and to all my friends, to Manolo Montesinos,[4] and, especially, to the great Manuel de Falla.[5] I have often spoken of him in New York, always with an enthusiasm and admiration he can scarcely imagine. I have seen so many things here, and yet I understand what an ex-

[4] Manuel Fernández-Montesinos, who married Federico's sister Concepción in 1929, was Mayor of Granada when the Civil War broke out. He was arrested in his office and executed by the Nationalists on August 16, 1936, several days before Lorca's own death.

[5] Lorca had known Falla since the composer had moved to Granada in 1920. Relations had been somewhat strained since December 1928, when Lorca published the first two sections of his unorthodox "Ode to the Most Holy Sacrament" in the *Revista de Occidente*, Madrid, with a dedication to Falla. Falla disapproved of the poem, and said so in a pained letter. See Francisco García Lorca, *In the Green Morning*, tr. C. Maurer (N.Y.: New Directions, 1986), pp. 127–28. Lorca completed the poem in New York in December 1929.

221.

traordinary man he is, and how we should all love him and encourage him in all he does.

Hugs and kisses to you from your son

Federico

August 8 [*1929*]

Dearest family,

My stay in New York goes calmly on, and I think I am getting a lot out of it. I am beginning to understand some English, a little bit, anyway, but I am translating, and I think I will win the battle in the end.

I have also begun to write, and think what I am writing is good. But of course I don't want to publish any of it until it is completely finished and polished.

They are typically American poems, and almost all of them deal with the blacks.[1] I think I will return to Spain with at least two books, although I have yet to see and study the most important aspects of all this.

I am deeply interested in New York, and think I can strike a new note not only in Spanish poetry but in all that has been written about these things. But don't tell anyone. It seems likely that once my book on New York is finished, it will be translated into English and published *first* in that language. My friend Brickell, the editor, wants to publish something of mine, and that is fine with me. The next time I write, I will send you two long articles about my poetry from one of the big New York daily newspapers, plus *Alhambra* magazine, which has published six photos of me (one of them of me sitting on the rim of the fountain at the baths in Lanjarón).[2]

---

[1] The manuscripts of "The King of Harlem" and "Standards and Paradise of the Blacks" are dated August 5 and August 12, respectively.

[2] See letter of July 6, *n.* 9.

Naturally, all this is in English—Paquito will do the translating.

About Paquito, what can I say?[3] I know Father must have been sorely disappointed, for he wanted Paco to be *bolder*. But it must be all over by now, and you are probably feeling happy and thankful. I approve completely of Paquito's attitude. Any honorable, truly conscientious man would feel the same way. I would have done the same thing myself. And besides, next year Paquito will do magnificently on the exams. He will no longer be nervous, and he'll know the subject matter backwards and forwards. I am very sorry about the whole thing—on his account, not yours, for in the end, of course, he will accomplish whatever he wants to. But I feel sorry for him: perhaps he will begin to feel depressed, and that would be a shame for a boy of his genius, elegance, and extraordinary intelligence. You ought to realize that Paquito is one of the most gifted, sensitive, levelheaded people I have ever met. And you ought to let the matter drop for now, and not badger him. I know that you won't, and that you'll feel happy with him. Tell him to work hard for the next time. I imagine you all feel happy to be back together again, and I would be, too, if I weren't so far from you. If I didn't have the friends I do in New York, this separation would be very sad indeed, but, to be honest, I have hardly had the chance to feel lonely. Maroto, who is a great tease, tells me, "No matter where you go, you're always the spoiled child, always the center of attention. It's no fair. Where you are, no one else exists." To be honest, I have some very good friends, and thanks to them my life has been interesting. Last night I went to a party at the home of Miss Adams, who is from one of the most distinguished families in

[3] Federico's brother had withdrawn from the examinations.

223.

New York. It was a party in my honor—she wanted to introduce me to her friends. There were a lot of nice Americans. An excellent pianist played music by Albéniz and Falla, and the girls wore embroidered Spanish silk shawls. In the dining room a surprise awaited us: bottles of sherry and Spanish brandy. I had a wonderful time. Naturally, I had to do my "Spanish song" number, and I played the guitar and sang *soleares*[4] with great success. I don't even worry about making a fool of myself, for I have never seen kinder, more innocent . . . and more intelligent people. The Adams family must have spent a small fortune on the party. When I said goodbye to them, and thanked them, they told me, "None of this can compare with all you did in Granada for our daughter." Miss Adams is truly charming. She has begun to make a name for herself, and is one of the most frequent contributors to the *Times*, the most important newspaper in all North America. I think Paquito met her in Granada.

It's interesting to see what prestige Spain enjoys in this country. In good society, a Spaniard is always considered a gentleman. Spain has a certain historical prestige and it's quite true that they always distinguish between us and the Spanish Americans.

I had a visit from Cecilio Huertas, a typical character from Fuente Vaqueros,[5] and an excellent person. We went out for a walk and chatted for a while. One of these days I'm going to visit him and have a *paella*, which a friend of his will make. He lives among Italians, and once in a while he lets out an Italian expression. His local accent is unchanged, but he sometimes comes out with things like "una dollare" for one dollar.

[4] A variety of *cante jondo* (flamenco). Lorca had been playing the guitar since 1921.

[5] The town where Federico was born.

He is so affectionate, he came to visit me last Sunday, but I couldn't attend to him, because two girls, friends of mine, had come to take me to the Russian church.[6] The Russian church is admirable. It's almost like the Catholic one. They have the Virgin and the saints, and the ritual is even more splendorous than ours. It is completely Byzantine, and more complicated and primitive than the Roman rite. But it is extremely beautiful, full of emotion. What are simply amazing are the choirs and the hymns. The Mass reaches its climax when the "pope," after consecrating the host, turns toward the audience, holds up the crucifix, and bursts into a loud lament with a beautiful melody. As theater, they really do it well, these "popes," with their long beards and glittering vestments. The ceremony lasted forever—one has to stand or kneel for over two hours, and they purified me with incense twelve or fifteen times.

The church was full of Russians and Greeks. Magnificent types. I saw the same old women one sees in Spain, kneeling before the Mother of Sorrows, or pounding their heads on the floor. The gestures of the faithful are more exaggerated than ours, for they are more Oriental, more vehement. They cross themselves backwards, extremely slowly, and they all carry candles and give evidence of extraordinary devotion. There is a devotion and (especially

[6] Sofía Megwinoff writes: "One Sunday we took him to the Russian (Catholic–Orthodox) church at the corner of Morningside Avenue and 120th Street . . . Federico was tense and frightened. We went on walking and entered a church in Harlem (black things were in vogue then). We went in when the Mass was beginning. Perhaps it was a Methodist church, I can't remember exactly. There he was *really* frightened. He stared at us and at the solemn black women, with their enormous eyes, many of them dressed in white, giving out papers with the hymns. Although no one seemed very surprised by our presence, Federico was frightened and anxious to escape" (Eisenberg, "Cuatro pesquisas," p. 15; my translation).

225.

in the part of the service devoted to the dead) a silence that one does not find in Spain.

But I still say that the beauty and profundity of Catholicism is infinitely superior. If one is going to be a practicing member of some religion, there is none more perfect than Catholicism.

What the Byzantine church has, and what I haven't found in Roman Catholicism, is this notion of the patriarch. The "pope" is a superior figure, emanating authority and goodness, a true patriarch, and our priests have none of that. The priest is a simple officiant, and as soon as he leaves the church, he can turn into the worst person imaginable. But, unlike the Catholic priest, the "pope" (whether because of the ritual or his vestments or his eminence) has the appearance of a superior man, one who has been initiated into mysteries.

I tell you all this because I think you will find it interesting. It will give you some idea of the number of different creatures and opposing beliefs that exist in this huge city, where life is so violent and so full of new reactions and secrets. Even so, I have finally begun to understand the layout of New York. I often go places by myself now, the only way to see things well, without hearing someone else's comments and opinions.

Next week my Russian friends and I are going to go to the Chinese theater, something I await with great interest.[7]

In a few days [sic] I leave for the Canadian border, the state of Vermont, where I'm going to spend fifteen or twenty days with a boy I met at the Residencia. He has a farm in the mountains on Lake Eden, and that is where I'm going. I'll write you from there, and you write to me there. Fifteen days is nothing. This trip is like going from

[7] Lorca seems to be referring to the Sun Sai Gai Company, who performed in the Grand Street Theater.

226.

Granada to Loja, and yet it involves a twenty-hour train ride. You simply can't imagine the immensity of the United States.

This boy, who is a poet, was so eager to have me visit him that he sent me the $20 train fare. I've asked my friends if this is normal, and they tell me it is the custom here. When an American invites you, he treats you to *everything*. So, next week I take the train to Burlington, and I expect to have a great time. This boy is extremely kind, and in his house only English is spoken, which will be very good for me. But to give you some idea of the freedom of belief in this country, let me just tell you that the mother of this boy is a fervent Catholic, the father a Protestant, the boy himself a Catholic, and a cousin who lives with them is a complete atheist and a demagogue. They get along like angels.[8]

Mother, you asked how I was spending my time, and how much money I am spending. The first few days I spent more, out of necessity. But by now I'm living very, very simply. Simply but well. I pay seven dollars a week for the room, which is a good one. As for food, that depends. I eat in the dining hall at John Jay for 55 cents, and the food is quite good. When I am hungrier, I spend 75 cents. When I go downtown and eat with friends, it is about a dollar.

Laundry is very expensive, a dollar or a dollar and a half to have my clothes washed, and that's why I'm being so careful with them. I haven't had to make the slightest

[8] Cummings calls this a "fantasy." "My family [were] born Congregationalists, and you can't get much more Protestant than that. Mother was a churchly woman, but other than an occasional funeral or wedding, I don't think my father ever darkened the door of a church. There weren't even any Roman Catholics in the family. We had a cousin, daughter of my mother's sister, Edna Southwick, who with her mother visited us a week at the camp on Lake Eden. As I recall, Aunt Carrie and Edna were both Methodists" (letter to C. Maurer, March 1, 1984).

sacrifice. Of course, people are always inviting me to dinner, and I'm fortunate not to have to invite *them*, for I have no place of my own. The meals consist of soup, a platter of meat with potatoes, peas, beets, and sauces, a piece of cake or apple pie, a glass of iced tea with lemon, and a cup of coffee or a glass of milk. All this for 55 or 60 cents. There is plenty to eat, I couldn't eat more.

But I hope Father won't forget to send me my allowance right away, so I don't run short of money. He ought to do this right away. And please tell Paco to wire me whatever money I've earned from my books, so that I have money to go to the theater, which interests me enormously. The theater here is magnificent, and I hope to get a lot out of it for my own work. Goodbye, much love. Hugs and kisses from your son, who loves you and remembers you often.

Federico

Remember me to everyone, even when I forget to say so in the letter.

The weather continues to be excellent.

[*second week in August 1929*]

Dearest family,

Today I received Mother's letter, so I know Paco is back at the Huerta. Why doesn't he write me? I wrote him a long letter, and haven't gotten a reply. I asked him to send me books. *I still haven't seen my Canciones,*[1] and to me that doesn't seem right. Of course, I haven't written to the *Revista*, for I thought Paco would send it. But after what happened, I don't suppose he felt like it.

---

[1] The second edition of *Canciones* (*Songs*) was published by *Revista de Occidente* in 1929.

I haven't written to anyone because I haven't had time. In New York there is no time for anything. Since I have a lot of things to do, I spend all my writing time on you.

A moment ago I received a lovely photo, a bird's-eye (or airplane's-eye) view of the Acera del Casino. An American friend clipped it out of a Chicago newspaper and sent it to me right away, thinking our house would be in it. And indeed it is. In the center of the photo you can see the house, and the trees in the Plaza del Campillo. This was a touching little kindness. He also sends me all the articles on Spain which appear in the daily newspapers, and there are many of them.

The Americans are friendly, frank, and as open and disarming as children. They are incredibly naïve, and extremely helpful. This morning I was having breakfast with my friend Colin[2] on Wall Street, the center of business and banking, where the Stock Exchange is, and the huge skyscrapers.

It is the spectacle of all the world's money, in all its unbridled splendor and cruelty. I couldn't begin to describe the tumult and hugeness of it all—the voices, the shouts, the running to and fro, the elevators, the poignant, Dionysian worship of money. This is where one sees the magnificent legs of the typist who appears in so many movies, the charming, conniving wink of the gum-chewing office boy, the poor, pallid fellow who turns up his coat collar and timidly stretches out his hand and begs for a nickel. It is here that I have gotten a clear idea of a multitude fighting over money. It is a true world war, with a faint trace of courtesy.

We ate breakfast on the thirty-second floor with the president of a bank, a charming man with a depth of feline

[2] Campbell Hackforth-Jones (see letter of June 28, *n*. 9).

229.

coldness and ancient English reserve. People were coming in after being paid. They were all counting their dollars. Their hands were trembling as they always do when we are counting money. Out the window was the skyline of New York, crowned with great trees of smoke. Colin had five dollars in his pocket, and I had three. And he said in a truly charming way, "Just think. We are surrounded by millions. And yet the only two real gentlemen here are you and I." There was a *torrent* of noise on the street. When we left, I saw a man whose legs had been amputated, pushing himself in a little cart down one of the canyons between the buildings, and, a little way off, a madman talking to himself with a paper hat on his head.

Wall Street and its skyscrapers are truly marvelous. Several days ago I saw the Graf Zeppelin anchored beneath them like a green fish, and for a moment I thought I was dreaming.[3] Returning to the university is like returning to another country. It is completely quiet. The grass and the statues of Hamilton and Jefferson soothe me with their color and their broad faces of seventeenth-century revolutionaries.

I listen to the horns of the ships on the river, and if I want, I can imagine I am in the country. You probably think I am in a marvelous place, but I think that you are, too. You really are, you know. When you've seen New York, you've seen almost every city in North America. Everything is uniformly the same. But think of the variety one has in Spain! You travel "further" going from Granada to Gerona than crossing the entire United States.

[3] The German airship flew over Manhattan, on its way to Lakehurst, New Jersey, at nine in the evening on August 4, 1929, after a sixty-seven-hour transatlantic voyage.

Today's letter is but a greeting. Write me often. Ask the girls and Paquito to write me. Remember me to the rest of the family, to all my friends, and especially the Amigo family and the charming Joaquín Amigo,[4] who does not belie his name.

I think only you, and no one else, should read my letters. Just the family. But don't show them to *anyone* else, for they are personal letters, written for you and nobody else, and, besides, they have no literary value. They only matter as family letters. It would be ridiculous to think otherwise. Lots of hugs and kisses for all of you from

Federico

[*last week in August, 1929*]

Dearest Conchita and Isabelita,

Before leaving these woodlands, I am writing to you on a piece of bark which I myself pulled from the tree.[1] Lovely paper, isn't it? I got your letter, and Father's, and I hope you received mine from Eden Mills.[2] I'll send you the drawings.

Say hello to Manolo and everyone else.

Give Mother and Father and Paquito a kiss for me.

Hugs and kisses to you from

Federico

Now I'm going to stay with Ángel del Río, whose wife teaches me more English than anyone else. And then to John Jay Hall, Columbia University, for the semester.

---

[4] Joaquín Amigo Aguado, who had helped Lorca edit the literary magazine *gallo* in 1928.

[1] The letter is written in pen on a piece of birch bark.

[2] All three letters have been lost.

A big hug. I feel great. The meals here are a real challenge.

The title of this letter is "Autumn in New England."

[c. *September 21, 1929*]

Dearest Mother and Father,

I'm writing in pencil, for I'm changing dormitories and my room isn't ready yet. It has been a while since I last wrote. My summer vacation is over. After leaving Cummings, I spent a few delightful days with Ángel del Río.[1] In the morning I studied English and in the afternoon I worked.[2] And I have written a great deal: almost a whole book. I don't know why I say "almost": if I go on like this, I will return to Spain with three books. I had a great time with these friends of mine. They're my family here. Ángel's wife mends my clothes, ties my ties, and just about everything else. She's simply charming. She and her South American girlfriends *take care* of me: to them a poet is something fantastic. Then Onís came to get me, and drove me to his farm,[3] and I spent a week helping him with the Anthology he is preparing, a very important collection of the whole of Spanish and Latin American poetry. Follow-

---

[1] Del Río has described Federico's adventurous trip from Eden Mills, Vermont, to Bushnellsville, near Shandaken, New York, on August 29: "Lorca, finding himself alone in Kingston, had decided to take a taxi without being able to give the right directions to the driver. They had been going around mountain roads until a kindly neighbor had given them our address. The fare was $15. As Lorca had spent all his money, I had to pay the driver and placate his fury. Federico's terror was the outcome of his conviction that he was lost, without money enough to take care of the bill. Immediately he gave the incident a fantastic twist and said that the driver, whom he could not understand, had tried to rob and kill him in a dark corner of the woods" (Mildred Adams, p. 117).

[2] The untitled manuscript of "After a Walk" is dated "Bushnell-Ville (ESU) 6 de Septiembre 1929."

[3] Lorca spent September 18–21 at the home of Federico de Onís, Gardnertown Road, Newburgh, N.Y. (Eisenberg, "A Chronology," p. 238).

ing my own criteria, I myself selected the poems of Salvador Rueda, José Asunción Silva (a great Colombian poet), Machado, Juan Ramón, and some minor poets.[4]

Once I have moved in, I will have a new address—John Jay Hall, Columbia University—and that is where you should send your letters. All these trips have helped me get to know the admirable banks of the Hudson River. I have often sailed up and down it, and know all its villages and towns. And thus the East of the United States, the region least frequently visited by tourists, has become almost familiar to me. You can imagine how many amusing, and sometimes embarrassing, experiences I have had. I have discovered that I have a sense of humor that allows me to get through difficult situations. And I have a cold-bloodedness that comes from belonging to an ancient race, as compared with the "Samsonism" (children of Samson) of this people. My room in John Jay is wonderful.[5] It is on the twelfth floor of the dormitory, and I can see all the university buildings, the Hudson River, and a distant vista of white and pink skyscrapers. On the right, spanning the horizon, is a great bridge under construction, of incredible grace and strength.[6] The sky is magnificent, and the temperature is perfect. Autumn in New York is probably the loveliest season of the year, as it is everyplace else.

The university is full of joy and bustle. I must start to write my lectures. I already have the material for the

---

[4] *Antología de la poesía española e hispanoamericana (1882–1932)* (Madrid: Centro de Estudios Históricos, 1934). According to Onís, these poets (with the exception of Silva) were the ones whose presence is most noticeable in Lorca's first book, *Libro de poemas* (*Antología*, p. 1101).

[5] Room 1231.

[6] Construction work on the towers of the George Washington Bridge (then known as the Hudson River Bridge) was approaching completion in the summer of 1929.

first one, on "The Virgin in Alfonso the Wise and in Gonzalo de Berceo."[7] I am going to speak about the delightful Gothic Virgin in this place, where there are more Protestants than anywhere else in the world. (To me the word "Protestant" means *"dry" idiot.*[8]) I am amazed, and always chuckle to myself, to see how many sects and fake religious cults there are in this country. I can spot Catholics a mile off by their manner and their intelligence.

My lecture will be an apology for the Gothic faith, as it struggles against the sharp edges of the devil's world. I will write another one on "Adventure in Tirso and in Cervantes," and another, which is already completely thought out, on "The wind, the breeze, and the hurricane in sixteenth-century lyric poetry." A lecture on the breezy landscapes of certain poets, using the air as a touchstone to distinguish their temperaments and qualities.[9]

It seems likely I will soon make my trip as a lecturer, though I shudder to think of the macaws and parrots and rumba dancers that will be pounding on my shoulders and eardrums. But we'll see.

I will write again tomorrow or the day after. I have fallen a bit behind.

Your letters were waiting for me when I got back from Onís's house.

Tomorrow I will write to poor Encarnación. I was

[7] No fragments of this lecture have ever been found.

[8] A reference to those whom Lorca thought responsible for Prohibition. Cf. "The Birth of Christ," lines 19–20: "Idiot clergymen and cherubim in feathers / follow Luther in a line around the high corners."

[9] A fragment of this lecture, entitled "Escala del Aire" ("Ladder of Air"), has been found among Lorca's papers and published in *Federico García Lorca escribe a su familia*, pp. 129–30.

greatly saddened to hear of Mateo's death (may he rest in peace). He was extremely kind and affectionate. I plan to write them, but please give them my deepest condolences.

I will send Conchita the drawings she asks for, and write to Paco with all sorts of news. His letter made me realize how beautiful and wild the Monte del Duque must be. When I get back, we must go and see it. What Paco tells me about Estepona fills me with enthusiasm here in New York. How beautiful Andalusia is! And that seaside Andalusia . . . how refined and lovely. It is here that one realizes the beauty and importance of Spain. It is the only strong and vital country left in the world.

It seems likely I am going to Chicago, a nerve center of Yankee dynamism, and there I'll finish learning the value of the sea at Málaga and the little houses lost in the red mountains and the love and definitive grace of my own country. I have gone to the window. How I would love it if you could see this prodigiously impressive landscape of buildings and rivers, with the aristocratic university in the foreground, and the two magnificent granite fountains, with their cool water jets. And yet . . . I remember Polinario's tavern, with its cypress tree and broken chair.[10]

I feel wonderful. Hugs and kisses

Federico

P.S. I asked you for my October allowance because I must pay three months of the residence fee in advance. The room costs a dollar a day, and another dollar to eat makes two. This is paring expenses to a minimum, but I am getting

---

[10] A famous old tavern near the Alhambra, a meeting place for flamenco artists, run by the father of Lorca's friend the pianist Ángel Barrios.

by. That was the reason I asked for the money: so that I could pay in advance. Also, I've enrolled in an English course which I need to take.

I asked Ángel del Río for thirty dollars because I needed to have some money in the bank. The room is a good one, and this dormitory has a very inexpensive dining hall. Besides, it is the newest, most elegant dorm, and is prodigiously warm in winter. I have managed to live here on the same money as in Madrid. Sometimes, when I feel hungry, I spend a little more on food, but I want to eat less, because *I have put on weight*, and don't want that to happen.

I haven't received the money from the *Revista*. They have a lot of nerve. "Mun*cha* alma," as Ortega y Gasset[11] would say. I will save that money to go to the theater, which is very good and very new, and extremely interesting. So please, send the allowance at the beginning of each month. Send me my November allowance on the first of November.

Farewell.

Remember me to Montesinos and all my friends.

[*September 23?*]

Dearest Mother and Father,

Today I am nicely settled in. I have enrolled in my English class, and will audit several others. So *here I am*, a Columbia student. I asked you for my October allowance in order to pay for my room in advance, for that is what they require. Anyway, it is the best bargain in New York. I pay a dollar a day for the room. But the room is splendid,

[11] José Ortega y Gasset (1883–1955), the Spanish essayist who had founded the *Revista de Occidente*, publisher of Lorca's *Gypsy Ballads* and *Songs*.

236.

better than one could get for the same price in Spain. Clean towels daily, and they change the bed linens twice a week.

I live neatly and simply. They have invited me to give several lectures at universities in the West, and I'll almost surely go, for that way I will earn some money. Were it *enough*, I would write you, and you wouldn't have to send any more. Anyway, if I earn a few extra dollars, I will use them to buy some things and to go to shows, especially the theater.

This morning they began "initiating" the new students in my dormitory. At nine in the morning I was awakened by the shouting, went to the window, and saw them *stripping* the initiates—some of them down to their birthday suits. In five minutes there was a huge mound of shoes on the playing field. Two brave souls who put up a fight were seized without mercy and tossed into the basin of a fountain by the door of the library. The poor boys came out like wet hens; from up here they looked like two broken rag dolls.

It was great fun. Just across from me the eighteenth-century statue of Hamilton, about to break into a minuet or a gavotte, is wearing a paper hat and holding a huge broom. The students greet each other with long handshakes, exactly like the peasants of Asquerosa or Romilla.[1] They grip each other's hands and for a long minute or two they pump them up and down in an almost mechanical way. Others show their affection by feigning punches, and finish off with a big bear hug.

Everywhere, there are dull thuds, shouting, the noise of elevators, and red, blue, and green sweaters.

---

[1] Two villages near Granada where Lorca had spent much time as a young man.

Here's a surprise for you—my room is number 1231! My neighbor, who is a very refined person, a student from Georgia,[2] invited me in for tea a moment ago, and we conversed for the most part in sign language, for what is most difficult about English isn't reading, but listening, and listening is very difficult indeed. Many words which I can recognize when they are written down escape me completely when I hear them, because we say "a" and it *is* "a," but they pronounce the "a" in six or seven different ways, so it's a real mess. But I never despair, I only smile and I manage to make myself understood whenever I want. The hard part is getting them to recognize the word one is saying, a rather complicated matter, given the special *head* of the Anglo-Saxon race. Just now the Columbia rugby team[3] has come onto the field, dressed in their black and tobacco-colored uniforms. The players are a little like sandpaper and a little like tree trunks, and they are frighteningly strong and seedy-looking. Soon they will break each other's heads open and no one will care. The same thing holds true for rugby players as for picadors. Everyone secretly hopes the picador will be driven up against the wall, and feels let down if he does a good job with the *pica*—you've probably noticed how people applaud them with a certain

[2] No students from Georgia seem to have been living on the twelfth floor of John Jay. Lorca is probably referring to either Francis C. Hayes or John Crow, both Southerners. Crow remembers García Lorca as being "very much out of his element . . . As a matter of fact, he used to annoy me. I didn't realize at the time that he would be such a major figure. García Lorca was somewhat stuck on himself in the first place! He always talked about how great he was, which rubbed us the wrong way. The thing that bothered us most was that he'd come by our rooms saying, *'Vi la luz encendida'* ('I saw the light on'). He would knock on the door at about 2:00 in the morning when we were just getting ready for the next day's classes, and he would come sit down for a couple of hours until we were exhausted!" See Onofre di Stefano and Darlene Lorenz, "Conversations with three Emeritus Professors from UCLA," *Mester* VIII (1979), pp. 30–31.

[3] He means the football team. The character in *Once Five Years Pass* whom Lorca calls "Jugador de rugby" is really a football player.

anger. I love rugby, for besides being typically American, it is so exciting and has such *incredible* natural beauty that it gives me a lump in my throat. Of course, I could never have been a player. I am sending you some photos taken by del Río and his wife in the sort of cabin we lived in for a while. I think I look absolutely stunning. In one of the photos, I appear with Helen and Stanton, the children who went for walks with me in the woods. One day I asked Stanton, "Are there bears here, too?" and he answered, "Yes, sir, there are. There are bears and roosters and frogs and many little tiny bugs we can't even see." This shows his charming innocence—in a Spanish twelve-year-old, such a statement would be inconceivable.

In other photos, I'm with del Río and his wife. And there is one which Amelia took, catching me off guard while I was writing. She says this is the one in which I look "cutest."

Write me long letters, and give me news. I suppose the Procession of the Virgin is over by now, and all those fairs they hold in the village squares are going on, threatened, as always, by the rains.

I feel fine. Autumn in Lanjarón is wonderful. You must take Mother to Lanjarón whether she likes it or not. You must *make* her go, and if she hasn't gone, or isn't going, and has an attack of colitis, Paco and Conchita and Isabelita will be to blame, and I'll be angry with them for the rest of my life. Hugs and kisses.

                                                          Federico

                                                    [*October 21, 1929*]

Dearest family,

I have received your letters, and you mine. I'm feeling well, and hope that you are, too.

239.

All this is beginning to change a bit for me, for I now know how to get around this huge city. But it is only now, when I know how to move about and ask questions and shop by myself, that I realize how huge this city and this civilization are. You have to live here for a few months to finally grasp the layout of New York and its immensity, which goes unsuspected in the first few days.

The other day, at *last*, I really got lost. I went out to do some errands, and took the elevated train. But instead of the Sixth Avenue train I mistakenly caught the Ninth Avenue one, which took me in the wrong direction, to a place totally unknown to me. It was a huge city of low, wooden houses, full of Chinese people and signs in Chinese, with the muted music of player pianos and jazz orchestras. I realized I was lost, and I started to look around at the streets and browse in the Chinese stores. Lunchtime came, and I ate at a Chinese restaurant. For sixty cents I had a very strange, totally cold, but undeniably tasty meal. The little Chinese boy who waited on me couldn't have been older than ten, and he looked like a pretty doll. He was wearing a little red smock and he left the plates on the table with an almost reptilian silence, but in an exquisite, aristocratic way. Afterwards I went out and began to explore the city, a neighborhood about four times the size of Granada, and at last, since I knew I was lost, and had almost gotten lost on purpose, I began looking for the subway stops and the elevated train. But the stops I found weren't the ones I needed, and they would have led me even farther astray. I felt a certain anguish, as though I were in a virgin forest or on an island on some planet not my own. And I didn't want to ask directions. I had only to ask a policeman to point me in the right direction . . . and in the end I did have to ask for help. I saw some women going by and questioned them in English. And what a surprise! They answered in perfect Spanish: *"Venga con nosotros, que lle-vamos el mismo camino."*[1] They were two wealthy women from La Coruña who were passing through New York. You can imagine what a good laugh we all had. At last we took the elevated train and I got off at Columbia. But then I went back to the subway and reached the place I had wanted to go in the first place (a complicated matter), and I did what I had set out to do. By the time I got back to Columbia it was midnight. Until something like this happens to you, you just don't realize where you are, and how immense these streets are, and how many millions of people live here. Anyway, I am beginning to get to know the city. Please don't tell me to carry a map. The map never helps me at all, it's useless. When it comes to maps, I have no sense of direction. When I trust my instinct I reach my destination, but a map only leads me astray. I just don't have the knack for it. I had a terrible time learning which was my right hand, and in fact I still have to make the sign of the cross with it before turning right into a building or down a street. I don't know which is my right hand, just as I didn't understand the mystery of the clock until I was almost twenty years old. A map is just im-possible, for me at least: I can't seem to link its abstract lines with the living, noisy reality around me. But I do perfectly well without it, better than most people do with their special maps. My spatial memory is amazing. Once I have been somewhere, I remember it always, and my friends can't believe it when we're on the elevated train at night, and you can see hardly anything, and I tell them, "We're going by Eighth Street." But this isn't at all strange in New York, which, as I told you before, is quite easy to figure out. You don't get lost very often, and if you

[1] "Come with us. We're going in the same direction."

do, you can pick up the thread immediately. What *does* cause problems is its size, and it is truly surprising how *long* it takes to get from one place to another.

We are well into autumn now, and the light is very beautiful in the parks and on the avenues. The university is preparing to celebrate its anniversary, and in front of my dormitory they are putting up the speakers' platform. I practice my lousy English with my American friends. I understand *myself*, at least, and I go to their rooms, or they come to mine, to have tea. One of them is very impressed with the Spanish photographs of Isabelita and Conchita. I have never seen more innocent creatures in my life than these Columbia students, or kinder, or more savage ones. This is a totally savage people, perhaps because there is no class system. These boys stretch and yawn with the innocence of animals, they sneeze without taking out their handkerchiefs and are always shouting, everywhere. And yet they are open and friendly, and they truly enjoy doing a favor for you. But how different they are from Spaniards who have been brought up properly.

I have also been going to the rugby games at the stadium of the university. The day before yesterday, four players were knocked out cold.[2] I can understand how excited people get, for it is an amazingly beautiful, graceful, manly spectacle, with special appeal for the weakling who is unfit to participate.

A bullring is nothing compared to this—it is a scandal. What barbarians they are! I have never heard people scream and swear the way they do in these Anglo–Saxon crowds, laced with blacks and old Indians.[3]

[2] Lorca refers, with his usual exaggeration, to the Columbia–Dartmouth game of October 19, 1929.

[3] "Old Indians"? Perhaps Dartmouth fans wearing Indian headdresses. According to the *Times* of October 20, 1929, around forty thousand people attended.

Changing the subject, Paco wrote me a letter for which I am deeply grateful. But *I don't owe any money to anyone,* thank God. I haven't asked anyone for money because I have been leading a very frugal life, and don't want to be a burden. I have received my money from the *Revista,* and that was the money I used to register at the university.[4] I asked you to advance me my monthly allowance because I had to pay the residence fee in advance. I had more than enough money in the bank and was able to pay the fee, and still have money left over to pay for meals.

I asked Don Fernando for thirty dollars, I think, because I didn't remember how much I had, and it came in handy. And come to think of it, I don't believe I've asked you for any money beyond the monthly allowance we agreed upon. A hundred dollars isn't much, but my life is very simple. Don't send more. Well, perhaps twenty dollars more per month, but until now I have managed nicely. Besides, I am going to give some lectures, and will use that money to buy what I need.[5] If I need money urgently for anything, I'll ask for it. What you ought to do is to send the money at the beginning of the month directly to the bank where I have my account: Corn Exchange Trust Company, University Branch, Broadway and 113th Street. And of course, if I succeed as a lecturer, you won't have to send me anything at all. Well, perhaps fifty dollars.

A student can live on less money than anyone else in

[4] On September 27, Lorca paid the fifty-dollar matriculation fee for two English classes in the Columbia University Extension Division, but later withdrew (Eisenberg, "Cuatro pesquisas," p. 2–3).

[5] On January 21, 1930, Lorca gave a lecture on Spanish lullabies at Vassar College, and grudgingly accepted an honorarium of $75 (Andrew A. Anderson, "García Lorca at Vassar College: Two Unpublished Letters," *García Lorca Review* XI [1983], pp. 100–9). On February 10, he spoke at Columbia University (301 Philosophy Hall) on "Three Modes of Poetry: Imagination, Inspiration and Evasion."

the United States. Only here could I get by on one hundred dollars. We'll see whether my allowance will leave me enough to go to the theater, in which I am greatly interested. I have been writing a play which might prove interesting.[6] One must think of the theater of the future. Everything that now exists in Spain is dead. Either the theater changes radically, or it dies away forever. There is no other solution.

Write me often, and I will, too. I will end this and get to work. It is three in the afternoon, and the wind is blowing hard and whistling around the twelfth floor. The radiator is on, and it is so hot that I have to leave the top part of the window open a little. The heating system is amazingly good. Not that the old charcoal brazier doesn't have a certain charm, which I love, but it is barbarous when compared to these superb radiators.

Hugs and kisses to everyone.

Federico

[*October 22 or 23, 1929*]

Dearest Mother, Father, and Conchita,

The problem you mention in your letter has an easy solution. If you want me to return, you have only to send me a cable, and I will do so immediately. I would rather be here, of course, but I could always put my affairs quickly in order and leave. What I really ought to do is stay for at least another two months, if I am to take advantage of this.

But I will do whatever you say. I am willing to leave

---

[6] Probably *Así que pasen cinco años (Once Five Years Pass)*, which he would finish in summer 1931. For the text of this work, see William Bryant Logan and Ángel Gil Orrios, tr., in *American Theatre* III, no. 9 (Dec. 1986).

and, naturally, will be glad to see you. But it seems a good idea, since I'm already here, to stay a while longer, above all if I can earn some money, which seems probable. Conchita's wedding plans seem very natural, and I don't want to do anything to disturb them.[1] They make a happy couple, and everyone is fond of them, and since Conchita will remain in Granada, they won't have the emotional difficulty of separation. Her husband is our close friend, and we know him well enough to know what a good person he is, and what a gentleman. And besides, it seems very good, since Paco and I are such drones and haven't married and had children, that Conchita should form a family. I am very happy with the *rightness* of this marriage, and anyway, that is the way the world is today. Only God knows the truth. If I am not at the wedding (and that is up to you), you should write me and telephone me right away.

Some English friends of mine in New York have begun to see what they can do to have my theater performed here. This might be a good thing for me, and it would be excellent if it really happened.

If something is performed, it would be *Perlimplín* and *The Billyclub Puppets*, translated into English and done with a nice set.[2] There is avant-garde theater here, and it wouldn't be difficult. I don't want to get my hopes up: I'll just wait and see. It is the ladies who are taking an interest in all this. In fact, it is the women who do everything in America. One of them is a millionaire and there are also three

[1] Concepción García Lorca and Manuel Fernández-Montesinos were married on December 7, 1929.

[2] Mildred Adams had offered to translate *Amor de don Perlimplín con Belisa en su jardín* and the *Títeres de Cachiporra* into English. But none of Lorca's works was produced in New York until February 1935 (*Bitter Oleander* [*Bodas de sangre*] at the Neighborhood Playhouse).

or four Jewish women connected with the world of letters. I haven't done anything, but we'll see. Naturally I would love to be successful here. Not only would it advance my career, it would be beautiful to arrive in New York and have them perform what was shamefully banned in Spain or what no one wanted to put on "because there's no audience for it." But, as I said, I'm not getting my hopes up. We'll see. I will keep you posted. And don't tell anyone about this—as I said, it is still up in the air. But it might happen.

I received, unexpectedly, $140. Many, many thanks! You are too good to me, and Father is extremely generous. But I live simply, and am happy to say I haven't run out of money, and haven't had to ask anyone for a loan. I am more *responsible* than ever. It may seem hard to believe, but I spent more in Madrid than I do here. The life I was leading in Madrid was more dissipated and more pretentious. Here there are days when it is as though I were living in a small town. It is wonderfully peaceful.

Sometimes I go to the theater. I have seen a black revue which is one of the loveliest, most moving shows one can see, and I have become a fervent admirer of the talking pictures, for one can work true miracles. I would love to make a talking picture, and am going to try my hand at it, and see what happens.[3] It is at the movies that I learn the most English. Just last night I went to a Harold Lloyd movie, a talking film that was simply delightful.[4] In the

[3] While in New York Lorca did write the script for a short surrealistic silent film entitled "Viaje a la luna" ("Trip to the Moon"). The text may be found in *OC*, Vol. II, pp. 1139–48. An English translation was published by Bernice G. Duncan, *New Directions 18* (1964), pp. 35–41, and there is a fine study by Antonio Monegal, "Entre el papel y la pantalla: *Viaje a la luna* de F.G.L.," *Litoral* (Málaga) 174–76 (1987), pp. 242–58. The script was never filmed.

[4] "Welcome Danger," Harold Lloyd's first talking picture.

talkies you hear sighs, the breeze, and even the faintest sounds, all faithfully reproduced.

Write me at once and tell me how you are, what is going on, what you are thinking about. I am in good health, thank God.

Tomorrow I will write you a long letter and tell you lots of things. Today's letter is a bit short, not because I don't feel like writing, but because I don't like this paper. I am sending you a lovely photo taken alongside the sundial of the university. It is an enormous ball of porphyry. If you look at the ball very closely, you can make out a landscape of skyscrapers, and the sun.

I think I look pretty good. You can't say I don't send you enough pictures.

Remember me to everyone. Hugs and kisses and much love from your son, who misses you.

Federico

[*first week in November 1929*]

Dearest family,

How are you? I'm doing fine, thank God, in this enormous country, which seems stranger and stranger, ever more fraught with absurd, incredible things. The fall semester has begun, and New York is full of theater, film directors, opera, and automobiles. Every day they begin a new skyscraper: they are finishing one that is a hundred stories high, a black-and-white building that is truly marvelous.[1] I am still surprised by it all, but by now I've found my bearings, and can get around the city and its six boroughs completely on my own. What a pleasure to discover

[1] The Chrysler Building, which was opened to the public in April 1930.

things by myself, without needing anyone's help. There are moments, amid the urban landscape and all its strange sights, when I really miss you all.

A few days ago I had the pleasure (or the horror) of seeing the stock market collapse. As you know, the New York stock market is the stock market of the entire *world*. The crash means nothing to the international economy. But it was dreadful. Twelve *billion* dollars were lost! The sight of Wall Street, which I've already told you about (it is the center of the world banking industry), was indescribable. I spent more than seven hours mingling with the crowd when the panic was at its height. I just couldn't leave. Everywhere one looked, there were men shouting and arguing like animals and women crying. Groups of Jews were screaming and wailing on the stairways and on every corner These were the people who were ruined overnight. The messengers worked so hard running orders that many of them simply collapsed, and no one was able to wake them or get them on their feet. The streets—the terrible canyons between the buildings—were filled with hysteria and chaos, and you cannot possibly imagine the suffering and anguish of the crowd. Obviously, the more everyone panicked, the more stock prices fell. At one point the government and the great bankers had to intervene and try to bring everyone to their senses.[2] In the crowd, the screaming, the unbearable hysteria, I found a friend of mine, a woman who came up to me in tears because she had lost everything she had, about fifty thousand dollars. I tried to console her, as did her other friends. It was the same everywhere—people fainting, cars honking their horns,

---

[2] He is probably referring to the meeting that took place on October 24 at the offices of J. P. Morgan. In their report to the press, a group of bankers managed to convey the impression that the government would intervene, thus calming the public and keeping stock prices from falling still further.

telephones ringing. Twelve billion dollars lost. It is simply unbelievable.

When I broke away from that inferno, I found traffic cut off on Sixth Avenue. A banker had thrown himself out the window of his room on the sixteenth floor of the Hotel Astor. I got there just at the moment they were lifting the cadaver. He was a very tall red-haired man, and all I can remember is his huge floury white hands against the gray cement street.[3] This sight gave me a new vision of American civilization, and I found it all very logical. I don't mean that I liked it. But I watched it all in cold blood, and I am happy I witnessed it. It was a sight as horrifying as a ship going down, and there was a total absence of Christianity. I thought pityingly about all those people with their narrow, closed spirits, victims of the terrible pressure and cold, calculating refinement of two or three bankers who own the world.

After it was over, I went off in search of my Russian friends, who are so full of spirit, *crazy* almost, but open to all of life's rawness and mystery. One of these Russians

[3] There is no mention of a death at the Hotel Astor (Forty-fourth and Broadway) in the New York papers for October 24 and 25. The death reported by Lorca was probably that of a man who fell or jumped from the fourteenth story of the Roosevelt Hotel (Madison Avenue and Forty-sixth Street) at 6 p.m. on October 24 (see "Wealthy Vermont Man Falls 14 Stories to Death Here," *New York World*, Oct. 25, 1929, p. 20). Four years later, in Argentina, Lorca told a journalist: "I was lucky enough to see the latest 'crash,' a formidable sight . . . It was a painful, yet a great experience . . . A friend of mine told me, and we went to see it . . . That day I saw six [!] suicides . . . We were going down the street and suddenly a man threw himself from the enormous building of the Hotel Astor, and was crushed on the sidewalk" (*OC*, Vol. III, p. 543). Lorca's report of six suicides is not entirely inexplicable. The *Times* reported: "Wild rumors of failures, of suicides and other calamity spread through the district. Ambulances were reported clanging to buildings where men were reported to have shot themselves because of losses. Last night, when the hysteria had ebbed, all [!] of the rumors were demonstrated to have been just rumors" ("Weird Roar Surges from Exchange Floor During Trading," *The New York Times*, Oct. 25, 1929, p. 2).

(I have never told you about him) is among the most extraordinary men I have ever met.[4] He has twice been sentenced to death for his beliefs, and he lives here at Columbia as a student under an assumed name. He is twenty-seven years old, and knows ten languages. Sometimes he gives me English lessons, and he reads my poems with the enthusiasm only a Russian can feel. It seems he will soon leave, and return to his life as a revolutionary. Here, of course, he hasn't done anything, nor does he intend to. But what a great heart, and what intelligence! I'm enclosing a photograph of me with María Antonieta Rivas, a Mexican millionaire, founder of the magazine *Contemporáneos* and of the Ulysses Theater in Mexico City, a great friend of mine.[5] Also shown are a Hindu ballerina who is extremely pretty and a Hawaiian pianist who is very good and has been a great success in New York. They are three strange birds, to be sure, but all three are intelligent and very artistic.

The photo shows Columbia University, and we took it the same day as the one I sent you showing the ball in the background. You can't see my dormitory, but it's not far away. All the buildings in the photo are part of the university. These people came to get me three Sundays ago and we spent the afternoon together. That day I spent the whole morning at the Metropolitan Museum, which is marvelous, taking notes on the Virgins painted by the fourteenth-century primitives, for my study on Gonzalo de Berceo.

[4] Perhaps this is Vladimir D. Kazakevich, who lived near Lorca on the twelfth floor of John Jay Hall (*Men's Residence Halls Charge Sheets*, July 1, 1929–June 30, 1930, Columbiana Collection, Columbia University, Administrative Records, Cage 25, Range 3, section 9).

[5] María Antonieta Rivas (1900–31), who was reportedly in love with García Lorca, committed suicide two years later in Notre Dame Cathedral (Eisenberg, "A Chronology," p. 240).

Please write often and write long letters, and send me all the news, above all news of Conchita.

Remember me to all, especially to Manolo Montesinos. Hugs and kisses and much love from your

Federico

[*January 1930*]

Dearest family:

The Christmas season has gone by, with excellent weather and all its usual sparkle and glitter. I received your letters and the ones Manolo and Conchita sent me from Córdoba and Barcelona, which I deeply appreciate. They ought to celebrate their wedding now, since they weren't able to before. With a family as large as ours, it is hard to get everyone together long enough to celebrate *anything*. You see how Eloísa[1] recovered; so I hear from Conchita. Naturally, I'm delighted to hear she is better, and I'll feel even happier when she is back to normal. I hope you've had a very merry Christmas, the one you deserve.

On Christmas Eve I went to Onís's house for dinner. José Antonio Rubio was there, and Ángel and Amelia del Río, and the great Italian critic Prezzolini,[2] and his son Alessandro. The dinner was delicious, and there was plenty of wine and good cheer, but I had to leave them at ten o'clock to visit the Brickells, who had put up a Christmas tree and had invited all their closest friends. There I had an even better time, for it is another, very different society, and there I feel like a foreigner. They gave me an infinite number of presents, and I took part in a ceremony that is

[1] Federico's aunt, Eloísa Palacios García.

[2] Giuseppe Prezzolini was a member of the Committee on Intellectual Cooperation at the League of Nations, and a visiting professor in the Columbia University Italian Department.

251.

very English, but full of charm and warmth. They had set up a little altar and on some Talavera tiles they placed as many candles as there were guests. One by one, we lit them, and as we lit each candle, we had to make a wish for another person. Naturally, I wished for your health and happiness. One wish for the five of you (for you seem only one to me). The Americans take these superstitions quite seriously, for they are like children.

Afterwards we went to Midnight Mass at St. Paul's Church, where they sang a magnificent, stunningly solemn Mass with a choir of children.[3] And there I could see how alive Catholicism is in this country, for it must battle the Protestants and Jews, who have their churches right across the street. Hundreds and hundreds of people took Communion. It could be said that the entire cathedral took Communion. And it was a typical New York crowd: blacks, Chinese, Americans, etc.

But I know the best Christmas Eve I have ever seen was the one with the nuns at the Convent of St. Thomas, or that unforgettable Christmas Eve in Asquerosa, when they put a flat red hat on St. Joseph and a mantilla on the Virgin Mary.[4] But the excitement in the streets is the same. In all the city squares they put up Christmas trees covered with lights, and loudspeakers, and the people came and went, among the drunken sailors.

The next day *The New York Times* reported that there

[3] The church of St. Paul the Apostle, Columbus Avenue and Sixtieth Street.
[4] Federico told Brickell that St. Paul's was " 'the most beautiful church in the world, and the music, too, much better than anything he had ever heard in Spain.' Then he was taken to the Columbus Circle Childs for hotcakes and maple syrup, which invoked more ecstatic expressions, and he described another Christmas Eve in Spain when he and Maestro Falla had gone together to a little church somewhere in the hills near Granada, where the nuns danced stately dances before the high altar, playing castanets and tambourines" (Brickell, "A Spanish Poet," p. 391).

252:

were eighty cases of extremely serious alcohol poisoning, many of whom died, naturally.[5] Thanks to Prohibition, people drink more in New York than in any city in the world. There are hundreds of companies that try to sell alcohol and poison people, for they make wines from wood and from chemical substances that leave people blind or corrode their livers. It is dreadful! Of course, all this was imposed by the odious Methodist Church, which is much, much worse than the Spanish Jesuits ever were. In fact, the whole state of New York has never been "dry," but always wet, *very* wet, and all they have done is to make normal, clean drink a new, artificial paradise, longed for by everyone, and the number of drunks has risen sharply. Of course, I myself drink nothing without first making sure it is good. Besides, the homes I'm invited to are distinguished ones, and they offer high-quality drinks.

I am going to Cuba for sure in March. Onís has arranged the trip. I will give eight or ten lectures there. Would you please send me my lecture on Góngora? If you don't have a copy, I think Arboleya[6] does. I don't want to give it the way it is now, but will use it as a rough draft for the new one I'm writing. Also, please send the lecture on *cante jondo*. Not to deliver it as is, but to gather the ideas from it. This business of *cante jondo* and Andalusian poetry is an extremely important subject, and I am going to present it *polemically* not only in Cuba but afterwards in Madrid.

I am working hard. I am writing a book of poems, an interpretation of New York, and its forcefulness has made an impression on my friends. I think everything of mine grows pale alongside these latest poems, which are, so to

[5] See "75 Felled by Liquor, No Holiday Deaths," *The New York Times*, Dec. 26, 1929, p. 1.

[6] Enrique Gómez Arboleya, a friend who had helped Lorca launch the literary magazine *gallo*.

253.

speak, *symphonic*, like the noise and complexity of New York.

Greetings to everyone, the whole family, Eduarda,[7] and especially Aunt Isabel. Hugs and kisses for the girls and you.

Federico

You promised to tell me about the wedding, but you haven't told me anything I couldn't imagine for myself, or didn't know already.

Hugs and kisses.

[*Havana, April 5, 1930*]

Dearest Mother and Father,

My lectures have been very successful. Tomorrow I give the one on *cante jondo*, using gramophone records for the musical selections. The one on lullabies was a great hit. I played the piano myself, and the young actress María Tubau (niece of the old actress of the same name) sang the songs admirably. Everyone is looking forward to the lecture on *cante jondo*. Many people have joined the Institute[1] just to hear me, and many others have asked me for tickets (which I am unable to supply). I have given tickets to two young sailors from Seville who came to the hotel to see me and to an old woman who sells lottery tickets—she was born in Córdoba and once sang in the flamenco cafés. I have written a new lecture on this subject, and consider it very stimulating and very polemical.

I have already been to two Cuban towns, Sagua and Caibarién, where I witnessed a crocodile hunt. I can see

[7] Eduarda Miranda Lorca, a distant cousin of Lorca's mother.

[1] The Institución Hispano Cubana de Cultura, which sponsored García Lorca's lectures on Góngora, Spanish lullabies, the baroque poet Pedro Soto de Rojas, "The Mechanics of Poetry," and *cante jondo*.

you all opening your eyes very wide. But it's true. And I had one of the best times of my life . . . though I must say it was a bit scary, and very dangerous. I saw dozens of crocodiles four or six meters long. The swamp at Zapata is teeming with these little creatures. There is a booming crocodile industry, with factories to tan the hides. This was an exciting and very amusing expedition—exciting because, if the boat had tipped over, I wouldn't be here to tell about it. Anyway, I made it through in fine shape, and the people I was with praised what they called my "cold-bloodedness."

As is my custom, I did not take part in the hunt, and was only a spectator. There was a wonderful moment when I saw forty or fifty of those monsters leap nervously into the water. A beautiful experience.

I will send you the newspapers. But it would take three or four hours to clip out all that has been written, and is still being written. Some of it is very nice, and all of it is extremely affectionate. I am going to give more lectures than I thought, and that is the proof of my success here.

The day before yesterday, I was given a reception at the Lyceum Club by all the most distinguished ladies of Havana. There I saw the most beautiful women in the world. This island has some extremely original, beautiful women, due to the drop of Negro blood that all Cubans have. And the blacker the better. The mulattas here have a superior beauty, distinction, and delicacy. This island is a paradise. Cuba! If you can't find me, look for me in Andalusia or in Cuba. The other day I went into a huge baroque patio, full of tiles and fountains, and began to chat with some very poor black children, to whom I gave a few coins. When I was about to leave, the mother of these children, a huge good-natured black woman, offered me a cup of tea, which I had to accept and which I drank, surrounded by all the blacks in the neighborhood. You can see how well I've been treated. But often I go off on my own through the streets of Havana, chatting with people and observing the life of the city. Chacón[2] has been wonderful to me, and in Caibarién it was he who introduced me to the public. Don't forget that, in America, being a poet means more than being a prince in Europe.

I'm feeling well. Hugs for everybody. And hugs and kisses for you from your son and brother,

Federico

---

[2] The Cuban literary critic José María Chacón y Calvo (*b.* 1893), whom Lorca had met in Seville in 1922. Chacón's introduction, "Lorca, poeta tradicional," was published in *Revista de Avance* (Havana) V, no. 45 (April 15, 1930), pp. 101–2.

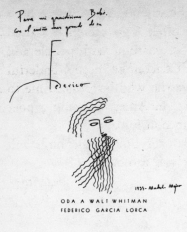

Para mi grandísimo Babe.
con el cariño mas grande de su

Federico

ODA A WALT WHITMAN
FEDERICO GARCIA LORCA

ALCANCIA MEXICO MCMXXXIII

NOTES ON
THE POEMS

Christopher Maurer

[Title page, *Oda a Walt Whitman*.
Non-commercial edition of fifty copies,
Alcancía, Mexico City, 1933]

The textual history of *Poeta en Nueva York* is extraordinarily complex, more so, perhaps, than that of any other book of poems in modern Spanish literature. Behind this complexity lies García Lorca's conviction that poetry, like theater, is as much an *oral* as a written phenomenon.

Lorca's generosity and impulsiveness, his habits as a writer, his inability to date his letters, keep his appointments, and take proper care of his papers, are factors which have had far-reaching effects on the publication of his works. His reluctance to have his poems and plays published is well known, almost legendary. He thought of his plays as works in continual evolution; when a play is published, that evolution is interrupted or broken off entirely. "Plays are meant to be heard in the theater. They ought to last as long as the performance lasts . . . This is what makes theater so beautiful. Scarcely has a play been created than it vanishes."[1] He had no wish, either, to see his poems "dead on the page"; even large public readings seemed to threaten them. "[I am a little afraid to read poems to so many people:] I am afraid my poems will stiffen and tremble like the dirty cats which children stone to death on the outskirts of villages."[2] In preparing his poems for publication Lorca was both painstaking and unmethodical. He sometimes gave away the autograph manuscript of a poem without making a copy, and he often relied on others to type his manuscripts or prepare handwritten fair copies. He did not always check the fair copies against the originals, and more than once he gave the latter to the typist (usually a friend, rather than a professional copyist) as a reward. His punctuation was idiosyncratic and his copyists were sometimes unable to decipher his handwriting or determine exactly what the poet himself had struck out or modified in the text. His statements to the press and to friends about work in progress, "completed" collections, and books "ready to be published" are not always reliable: PNY is a good example. Lorca's sudden death in 1936, the political climate of postwar Spain, the temporary exile of his family and some of his closest friends, the dispersion of his papers—all this has made it difficult to produce

[1] From an interview in 1935. *OC*, Vol. III, p. 640.
[2] Ibid, p. 360.

259.

faithful editions of his works. The textual history of *PNY* was complicated still further by García Lorca's changing, sometimes contradictory, intentions between 1930 and 1936 as to which poems to include, how to structure the book, what to title it, and where to publish it.

Poeta en Nueva York was published in 1940, four years after Lorca's death. There were two "first" editions: a bilingual one, with translations by Rolfe Humphries, published by W. W. Norton & Co. (New York), on May 1, 1940; and an edition in Spanish brought out by Lorca's friend, the writer José Bergamín, at Editorial Séneca, Mexico, approximately one month later. Both the manuscript used by Bergamín and all but a few pages of the typescript followed by Humphries are lost, and there is little hope they will ever be recovered. In 1972 a Spanish scholar, Eutimio Martín, drew attention for the first time to a number of troubling discrepancies between the Norton and Séneca texts, and set off an international debate that has lasted well over a decade. Researchers in Spain, France, Britain, Italy, and the United States have argued over the contents and character of the two missing manuscripts, the editorial roles of Humphries and Bergamín, and the question of how closely the structure of *PNY* and the text of certain poems follow Lorca's "final" intentions.[3] No satisfactory critical edition of *PNY* has yet been published; there is not even a consensus on whether such an edition is possible. The history of the debate itself need not concern us here. What does seem pertinent is a brief summary of the book's history, and some indication of the textual problems still under discussion.

[3] The most important contributions to this debate, and the ones most frequently drawn upon in this discussion, are: Eutimio Martín, "¿Existe una versión definitiva de 'PNY' de Lorca?," *Ínsula* 28, no. 310 (1972), pp. 1 and 10; Piero Menarini, *"PNY" di Federico García Lorca: Lettura critica* (Florence: La Nuova Italia, 1975); Daniel Eisenberg, *"PNY": historia y problemas de un texto de Lorca* (Barcelona: Ariel, 1976); Mario Hernández, "Notas al texto: *PNY*," in Federico García Lorca, *Antología poética*, 2nd ed. (Madrid: Alce, 1978); N. Dennis, "On the First Edition of Lorca's *PNY*," *Ottawa Hispánica* 1 (1979), pp. 47–83; Andrew A. Anderson, "Lorca's 'New York Poems': A Contribution to the Debate," *Forum for Modern Language Studies* XVII, 3 (July 1981), pp. 256–70; Idem, "The Evolution of García Lorca's Poetic Projects 1929–36 and the Textual Status of *PNY*," *Bulletin of Hispanic Studies* LXI (1983), pp. 221–46; and the works mentioned in the following notes.

260.

Almost all the poems in this book were composed in Vermont, New York, and Havana, Cuba, between early August 1929 and June 1930 (the dates are given by Lorca himself in the manuscripts), and some were extensively revised in the five years following his return from America. Lorca's lecture about *PNY* gave him the chance to "try out" many of the poems on audiences in Spain and Latin America, and the repeated readings of this lecture must have stimulated some of the revisions. The reading contains only eleven of the thirty-four poems later included in *PNY*: Lorca seems to have chosen the poems his audiences would understand with the least difficulty on a single reading and many of them were poems on social themes, with direct reference to the city itself: "Dance of Death," "The King of Harlem," "Standards and Paradise of the Blacks," "Landscape of a Vomiting Multitude," and "New York (Office and Denunciation)." Other poems may have been selected because they could be easily linked to a definite place ("Little Girl Drowned in the Well," "Double Poem of Lake Eden") or fit easily into the autobiographical narration.[4] In a word, the "book" which Lorca presented in public between 1932 and 1935 was meant to show (as he himself says in the lecture) his "lyrical reaction" *to the city* and to the United States. Absent from these readings was a more abstract and far more difficult series of New York poems, in which the city itself is only faintly if at all present. Here the major themes are love and death: "Cow," "Ruin," "Nocturne of Emptied Space," "Blind Panorama of New York," etc. There is firm evidence that in 1932, when he delivered the lecture for the first time, Lorca intended to publish *two* books, not one, related to the New York experience. One of the first reviewers of the lecture tells us that "the first, *Tierra y luna* [*Earth and Moon*], [is] more finely lyrical, with the same tender nostalgia of his *Canciones* [*Songs*]. The second, *Nueva York*, [is] powerful and hard-hitting, in a vein new and unknown to him."[5] While Lorca pondered which poems to include in these two collections, many of the New

---

[4] For a study of the lecture, see María Clemen Millán, "Sobre la escisión o no de *PNY* de Federico García Lorca," *El Crotalón. Anuario de Filología Española* 2 (1985), pp. 125–45.

[5] Quoted in Anderson, "The Evolution," p. 229.

York poems were printed in literary magazines and anthologies in Spain and Latin America.

By August 1935, his plans for *PNY* seem to have taken final shape: he announces that his secretary is typing the manuscript of "los poemas de Nueva York" ("the New York poems"). The news is found in a letter to a friend, Miguel Benítez Inglott, whom Lorca asks to send, "by return mail," the poem "Crucifixion," "for you are the only person who has it and I have no copy of my own."[6] The book, Lorca adds, will be published in October. Apparently, however, it took him another eight or nine months to bring this project to completion. In the spring of 1936, only months before his death, Lorca left his manuscript with Bergamín, director of the Madrid publishing house Cruz y Raya.[7] Bergamín and Lorca had arrived at some sort of oral agreement governing publication of *PNY*. The actual printing was to have been done by another friend, the poet Manuel Altolaguirre.

The manuscript given to Bergamín was a very unusual one:

[*It*] *was not a fully completed and fully typed manuscript, but rather a bulky hybrid affair, which contained hand-corrected printed cuttings, typescripts and hand-written fair copies (almost certainly not made by Lorca himself), a list of photographic illustrations, as well as reminder sheets indicating both where the missing texts of poems were to be located in the collection and where they were to be found (in magazines, with friends, etc.).*[8]

In place of the text of "Crucifixion," for example, Bergamín found the following note:

Poem number 3 of this part [section VII] is entitled "Crucifixion" and you must ask for the manuscript from Don Miguel Benítez, of the Fiat Company in Barcelona.

It seems likely that Lorca would have wanted Bergamín to review the manuscript carefully and keep a close eye on spelling and punctuation,

---

[6] García Lorca, *Epistolario*, ed. C. Maurer (Madrid: Alianza Editorial, 1983), Vol. II, pp. 164–65.

[7] See the prologue of Mario Hernández to his edition of *PNY* (Madrid: Fundación Banco Exterior, 1987), pp. 15–16.

[8] Anderson, "The Evolution," p. 237.

perhaps to retype it; and that the poet would have made further revisions, if not on the manuscript, then in the proofs. But the two writers never had the chance to meet again. García Lorca was assassinated in Granada in August.

Bergamín went to Paris in 1938, and from there emigrated to Mexico, where he established Editorial Séneca, with the intention of publishing books representative of the ideals of Republican Spain. It was in Paris that he seems to have made the copy of PNY which he later sent to Rolfe Humphries, editor and translator of the Norton edition. This copy seems to have been reasonably faithful to the original which Lorca had given to Bergamín in Madrid, and Humphries followed it with extreme care. The erratic punctuation and occasional misspellings in the Norton text are often attributable to Lorca himself. For several reasons, Humphries was an unusually accurate copyist: he had been trained as a classicist (in fact, he was a Latin teacher), and was familiar with the problems of textual scholarship. His command of Spanish was quite limited, far too uncertain to allow him to meddle with the orthography, punctuation, and textual incongruities of the copy sent to him by Bergamín.[9] He felt rather uneasy about editing a surrealist text, and was hesitant to attribute to textual error what might be construed as poetic freedom. Humphries himself says in the Translator's Note of the Norton edition:

The Poet in New York [sic] *came to me in typescript, not always perfectly clear and at times declaring its own confusion. I have followed the typescript as closely as I could, sometimes when I was not too sure it made sense—who can always tell, in surrealist poetry?—but there are some instances when I have had to try to establish the text. This has not been easy, for the versions of the few published poems do not by any means coincide. Lorca seems to have been a quick reviser, and there is no principle of objective epigraphical logic that the scholar-by-necessity can apply to extremely subjective surrealist stuff.* [p. 17]

Bergamín proceeded rather more boldly. Not only did he and his copy-editors normalize Lorca's punctuation and spelling, they eliminated some

---

[9] The history of Humphries's translation is thoroughly examined in Eisenberg, "PNY": historia y problemas.

of the dedications of individual poems, emended the text of certain poems, using published versions unavailable to Humphries, introduced stanza breaks where (presumably) none had existed in the original given to Bergamín by Lorca, and inserted four of Lorca's drawings, not all of which have any direct bearing on *PNY*.[10]

Most modern editions of *PNY* have followed the Bergamín/Séneca text. Two recent editors, Martín and Miguel García-Posada, have chosen a different, more controversial approach. While studying the New York manuscripts in the Lorca archives, Martín discovered a list made by Lorca in mid-1933[11] of seventeen poems he wished to include in *Tierra y luna*. Ten of these were later published in the Norton and Séneca editions of *PNY*, and three in *Diván del Tamarit*, an unrelated collection of Lorca's late poetry:

Tierra y luna
Cielo vivo
Nocturno del hueco
Asesinado [Asesinato?]
Templo del cielo [Panorama ciego de Nueva York]
Pequeño poema infinito
Luna y panorama de los insectos (poema de amor)
Muerte
Vaca
Encuentro [Canción de la muerte pequeña]
Ruina
Canción de las palomas [Casida de las palomas oscuras]
Vals en las ramas
Amarga [Gacela de la raíz amarga]
Paisaje con dos tumbas y un perro egipcio [sic]
Toro y jazmín [Casida del sueño al aire libre]
Omega

[10] See drawings nos. 166, 169, 179, and 184 and commentary in Federico García Lorca, *Dibujos*, ed. Mario Hernández (Madrid: Museo Español de Arte Contemporáneo, 1986).

[11] Anderson, "The Evolution," pp. 230–31.

Lorca had mentioned this project on several occasions between 1930 and 1933, and there is an additional mention of both *PNY* and *Tierra y luna* in an interview given in early 1936. *PNY*, Lorca declares,

has been finished for a long time. I have read fragments from it on a number of occasions. It will be three hundred pages in length, or a bit more. It will be a book big enough to knock someone's head off. It is already typed, and I think that in a few days I'll take it to the publisher. It will have photographs and movie stills as illustrations.[12] *Readers who drool lasciviously over "La casada infiel" ("The Unfaithful Wife"), and see only sensuality in my ballad, will feel cheated by* Poeta en Nueva York, *a sober book in which the social element plays an important role.*[13]

In the same interview, Lorca declares that he has finished *Tierra y luna*, and in view of these statements and the above list, Martín and García-Posada maintain that the author's last-known intentions may best be served by editing the two books separately. The canon of *Tierra y luna* should follow the list, and *PNY* should include only those poems Lorca read, or alluded to, in his lecture. This canon was adopted by Martín in his edition of 1981 and by García-Posada, with certain modifications, in 1982. Martín also does his best to show that the "bundle of documents" presented to Bergamín by Lorca in the spring of 1936 was manipulated, tinkered with, and "re-elaborated" by Bergamín well beyond the limits of normal editorial practice.[14]

Several recent contributions to the debate have shown the two-book

[12] Humphries states in his Translator's Note of 1940 (p. 17): "The typescript indicates that a selection of photographic illustrations was projected for the original book; it is impossible to reproduce them in this volume, but the list might be interesting to record—Statue of Liberty; Students Dancing, Dressed in Women's Clothes; Burnt Negro; Negro in Dress Suit; Wall Street; Broadway 1830 [a misprint for 1930?]; Crowd; Desert; African Masks; Photomontage of Street with Snakes and Wild Animals; Pines and Lake; Rural American Scene; Slaughterhouse; The Stock Exchange; The Pope with Feathers; Photomontage of the Head of Walt Whitman with His Beard Full of Butterflies; The Sea; Havana Landscape."

[13] *OC*, Vol. III, p. 678.

[14] Martín, pp. 55, 73–74.

theory to be untenable.[15] One important detail has been overlooked by Martín and other critics. It does not seem plausible that Bergamín would have invented the titles and dedications of the ten sections into which *PNY* is divided. Section VIII, "Two Odes," is dedicated "To my publisher, Armando Guibert": Lorca is alluding to a selection and translation of his poems which Armand Guibert—affectionately referred to by the poet as Armando—edited in Tunis in 1935, and this suggests that the section headings were devised before the manuscript ever reached Bergamín's hands. Section VII is entitled "Return to the City" and is dedicated to Lorca's friend Antonio Hernández Soriano, who had translated *Primeras canciones* (1936) into French. There is a letter from Soriano to Lorca, dated April 9, 1936, in which he speaks of accompanying Lorca back to New York (the poet was planning to stop there briefly on his way to Mexico, but he never made the trip). The dedication of "Return to the City" to Soriano would, therefore, have been especially appropriate. On the title page of section III ("Streets and Dreams") is an epigraph from a poem ("Vida") from Vicente Aleixandre's *La destrucción o el amor* (*Destruction or Love*), 1935. Such evidence that the book was structured by Lorca himself, in late 1935 or early 1936, is ignored by Martín; in fact, the section headings disappear in his edition.

There are other equally important reasons for rejecting the two-book theory espoused by Martín and García-Posada. The idea of deducing the canon of *PNY* from the text of the lecture has been questioned by Anderson and Millán. It is difficult to see how a book "big enough to knock a person's head off" could have been conjured up from the small number of poems actually read, or explicitly alluded to, during the course of the lecture. It is obvious that in deciding which poems to read, and in what order, Lorca must have been bound, in part, by the limitations and requirements of the genre itself, and it seems logical to suppose that he might have wanted to add other poems when the book

[15] See Anderson's review of the editions of Martín and García-Posada in *Revista Canadiense de Estudios Hispánicos* IX, no. 1 (1984), pp. 112–31; his "*PNY* una y otra vez," *El Crotalón. Anuario de Filología Española* 2 (1985), pp. 37–51; and María Clemen Millán, "Sobre la escisión."

was published; i.e., when he was no longer facing the time constraints of a poetry reading. The "Ode to Walt Whitman" was never included in the lecture, but there is firm evidence that Lorca wished it to be part of *PNY*.[16] "Nocturne of Emptied Space" appears on the *Tierra y luna* list, but was published in October 1935 as "From the unpublished book *Poeta en Nueva York*." By the time Lorca gave the 1936 interview, other poems from the list had been set aside for inclusion in *Diván del Tamarit*. There is no mention of *Tierra y luna* between 1933 and the 1936 interview. What that book had become by 1936 shall forever remain a mystery.

It will be apparent from the above summary that the Norton edition is closer to Lorca's original than the Séneca edition, and that there is no compelling reason to divide the book into two series of poems. The present edition follows the best modern one available, that of Mario Hernández.[17] Hernández uses Norton as a copy-text for all but one of the poems, but punctuates the poems in accordance with modern usage and corrects numerous errors which have been brought to light by recent textual scholarship. The Hernández text has been checked carefully against Norton, Séneca, and copies of the autograph manuscripts in the Lorca archives. Most departures from Hernández are indicated in the following notes, the purpose of which is to give the dates and first publications of the poems and, above all, to explain the editor's decisions with regard to certain problem areas in the text. In order to keep these notes as brief as possible, no mention is made of problems of punctuation, spacing, and stanza distribution. Discussion of these matters may be found in the editions already cited.

[16] Anderson, "Lorca's 'New York Poems,' " p. 265.

[17] Other poems written in 1929–30 but not forming part of *PNY* will be published in a future volume. The prose poem "Amantes asesinados por una perdiz," which is mentioned in Humphries's typescript, has also been omitted.

EM F.G.L., *Poeta en Nueva York / Tierra y luna*, ed. Eutimio Martín (Barcelona: Ariel, 1981).

GP ———, *Poesía, 2. Obras II*, ed. Miguel García-Posada (Madrid: Akal, 1982). All references are to *GP*'s notes to the text, pp. 719–38.

H ———, *Poeta en Nueva York*, edición y prólogo de Mario Hernández (Madrid: Fundación Banco Exterior, 1987).

Ms. Manuscript in the Fundación Federico García Lorca, Madrid. Most of the *PNY* manuscripts are reproduced in facsimile in Eutimio Martín, "Contribution à l'étude du cycle poétique newyorkais de Federico García Lorca: *Poeta en Nueva York, Tierra y luna* et autres poèmes (Essai d'édition critique)" (2 vols., unpublished doctoral dissertation, University of Poitiers, 1974).

N ———, *The Poet in New York and Other Poems of Federico García Lorca*, tr. Rolfe Humphries (New York: W. W. Norton, 1940).

S ———, *Poeta en Nueva York*, ed. José Bergamín (México: Editorial Séneca, 1940).

Vuelta de paseo / After a Walk. Unpublished during Lorca's lifetime.

1910 (Intermedio) / 1910 (Intermezzo). Unpublished during Lorca's lifetime. Variants: line 15 silencio de cangrejos *N, S*; silencios de cangrejos *Ms.* Line 19 cuando buscan su curso *N, S*; cuando buscan su pulso *Ms.* ("seeking their pulse"). In both cases, *GP* considers *N* and *S* to be in error.

La aurora / Dawn. Unpublished during Lorca's lifetime. *N* prints the poem without stanza breaks, and there are none in the *Ms.* either. In the *Ms.* Lorca has rejected two titles: "Obrero parado" ("Unemployed Worker") and "Amanecer" ("Daybreak"). The *Ms.* is undated, but the first title suggests it was written after the crash of the stock market in October 1929. Its position in the book is a matter of dispute. In *S* it is the ninth and final poem of section III; in *N* it is the third poem in section I. The order in *S* is suspect because no other section has more than five poems. *H* follows the order given in *N* and observes that, although thematically "Dawn" is not clearly related to the other poems in section I, Lorca might have placed it there (1) to emphasize, from the very outset, the idea of suffering, and (2) to draw early attention to the presence of the city. *H* also cites the poem's metrical similarity to other poems in section I. See also Anderson, "The Evolution," p. 240.

Tu infancia en Menton / Your Childhood in Menton. For stylistic reasons, *GP* believes this poem may have been written before Lorca's trip to New York. The title refers to a town on the French Riviera. The epigraph is from Jorge Guillén's poem "Los jardines" ("The Gardens") in section three of *Cántico*, 1928. The poem was published in *Héroe* (Madrid) 4 (1932), pp. 4–5, and in *Sur* (Buenos Aires) VII, no. 34 (July 1937), pp. 29–31, with the title "Ribera de 1910." The poem does not appear in *N*, for Humphries was unable to locate the text: he had only a reminder sheet reading: "Poem number 4 of this section is the one entitled 'Ribera 1910' published in *Héroe*. The new title is 'Tu infancia en Menton' " (translation mine). In his Translator's Note (p. 17) Humphries writes that it was "intended to be the fourth poem in the second section." In *S* it is the fourth poem in section *one*. Anderson believes that the poem must indeed have belonged to section one, for the reminder sheet is page 12 of Humphries's typescript. ("The Evolution," p. 240; see also Eisenberg, *"PNY": historia y problemas*, pp. 124–26.) Variants: line 9 hombre de Apolo *S*; hombro de Apolo *Sur*. If, as *GP* and *EM* maintain, *Sur*'s reading is the correct one, the line should read: "I gave you a norm of love, [a] shoulder of Apollo." Lines 18, 39 que no te entiende *S*; que no entiende *Sur*. *GP* believes this change was authorized by Lorca; the lines would read: ". . . which does not understand."

Fábula y rueda de los tres amigos / Fable of Three Friends to Be Sung in Rounds. Unpublished during Lorca's lifetime. Lorca's friend Rafael Martínez Nadal believes Lorca is remembering his love affair with Emilio Aladrén (Emilio) and adds coyly that he could identify the other two "friends" without difficulty. See *Cuatro lecciones sobre Federico García Lorca* (Madrid: Fundación Juan March/Cátedra, 1980), p. 30.

Norma y paraíso de los negros / Standards and Paradise of the Blacks. Unpublished during Lorca's lifetime. Two manuscripts are extant, one dated August 12, 1929, and a handwritten fair copy on the back of which Lorca wrote "para componer" ("ready to be typeset"). In the earlier *Ms.*, Lorca rejects two titles: "La luna desierta y as de bastos" ("Deserted Moon and Ace of Clubs") and "Paraíso quemado" ("Burnt Paradise"). The word "Paradise" may allude to the black cabaret, Smalls Paradise, mentioned in the lecture on *PNY*, and "*Burnt* Paradise" could be a reference to the persecution of the blacks by whites: one of the photos which Lorca wanted to include in *PNY* was a remarkable picture of a "burnt Negro" (*EM*, p. 95).

El rey de Harlem / The King of Harlem. First published in *Los cuatro vientos* (Madrid) 1 (Feb. 1933), pp. 5–10, as "Oda al Rey de Harlem." For the textual variants of *N* and *S*, see *GP*, pp. 723–24. The manuscript, dated August 5, 1929, is reproduced in facsimile in Martínez Nadal, *Autógrafos, I, Poemas y prosas* (Oxford: Dolphin Book Co., 1975), pp. 218–37.

Iglesia abandonada (Balada de la Gran Guerra) / Abandoned Church (Ballad of the Great War). First published in *Poesía* (Buenos Aires) I, no. 7 (Nov. 1933), pp. 28–29. The *Ms.* is dated November 29, 1929. *EM* and *GP* disagree on whether or not this poem should be included in section II. *GP* believes it has nothing to do with the other two poems about the blacks, and is related thematically to the poems of section I evoking Lorca's childhood. John K. Walsh notes that "Lorca might well have known the glowing legend of the Harlem blacks in the Great War: the record in Europe and the great parade of the 369th regiment (the 'Hellfighters') up Fifth Avenue . . . It is possible that the grief in the [father's] voice is from the lost promise of Harlem and its Blacks" (J. K. Walsh, "The Social and Sexual Geography of Lorca's *PNY*," read at a symposium on García Lorca at UCLA, May 2, 1986).

Danza de la muerte / Dance of Death. First published in *Revista de Avance* (Havana) V, no. 45 (April 15, 1930), pp. 107–9 (*Av*). Variants: line 66 los que crecen en el cruce *S*; los que duermen en el cruce *Av*, *N*, *H* ("who *sleep* where thighs and hard flames intersect"). In the archives is a clipping from *Av* with Lorca's handwritten revisions; the reading "duermen" is allowed to stand. In line 27, *GP* and *H* correct an error ("desfiles") in *N* and *S*. The correct reading is *perfiles* (contours, profiles).

Paisaje de la multitud que vomita / Landscape of a Vomiting Multitude. Published in *Poesía* I, no. 7 (Nov. 1933), pp. 25–26, and in *Noreste*

(Zaragoza) 11 (1935), p. 6. There are two extant manuscripts, the earliest of which is dated December 29, 1929.

Paisaje de la multitud que orina / Landscape of a Pissing Multitude. Unpublished during Lorca's lifetime. Variants: line 39 de alambradas *Ms.*; deslumbradas *N, S, H.* I have restored the *Ms.* reading; it would be easy for a copyist to mistake "de alambradas" ("of wire") for "deslumbradas" ("dazzled").

Asesinato / Murder. There are no less than five versions of this poem: *N, S*, a manuscript in the family archive, the text included in the lecture on *PNY* (which Lorca crossed out at an unknown date), and the text in *Cristal* (Pontevedra) II, no. 7 (Jan. 1933). For a comparison, see *EM,* pp. 261–62.

Navidad en el Hudson / Christmas on the Hudson. Unpublished during Lorca's lifetime. The *Ms.*, entitled "Navidad" ("Christmas"), is dated December 27, 1929.

Ciudad sin sueño / Sleepless City. Published in Gerardo Diego, *Poesía española. Antología: 1915–1931* (Madrid: Signo, 1932), pp. 320–22. The *Ms.* is dated October 9, 1929, and bears the title (crossed out by Lorca) "Vigilia" ("Vigil").

Panorama ciego de Nueva York / Blind Panorama of New York. Unpublished during Lorca's lifetime. The undated *Ms.* was originally titled "Templo del cielo (canto del espíritu interior)": "Temple of the Sky (Chant of the Inner Spirit)." Variants: line 9 muchachas heridas *Ms., EM, GP;* muchachos heridos *S, N, H.* The *Ms.* clearly reads muchach*as* ("girls"), and I take this to be the correct reading. On the back of the *Ms.* Lorca jotted the words, "Pájaros / gemidos / cielo interminable / [y el verdadero dolor alejado para siempre de nosotros]": "Birds /moaning / endless sky / [and true pain, forever distanced from us]." The words in brackets are crossed out.

Nacimiento de Cristo / The Birth of Christ. Unpublished during Lorca's lifetime. The undated *Ms.* includes only the first four stanzas. Variants: line 11 la mula tiene *Ms., N*; la luna tiene *S, H. GP* follows *N* but wonders whether the different readings might not be the result of indecision on Lorca's part (Bergamín's manuscript may have contained both variants, neither crossed out). The moon, *GP* argues, might be a metaphor for the sterile mule. *Mula* (mule) seems more likely, and is

271.

offered here, given the enumeration of other animals in the same stanza. Line 14 espinas *N, H*; espigas *S. Espinas* (thorns) seems a better reading than *espigas* (ears of wheat): the poet might be referring to the three nails of the crucifixion and, indirectly, to the crown of thorns.

Poema doble del Lago Eden / Double Poem of Lake Eden. First published in *Poesía* I, no. 7 (Nov. 1933), pp. 26–28. A manuscript submitted in 1930 to the *Revista de Avance*, but not published, is reproduced and discussed in Juan Marinello, *Contemporáneos: Noticia y memoria* (Havana: Universidad Central de las Villas, 1964), pp. 218–25 (*Ms. Av*). Lorca's misspelling of Eden ("Edem"), the lake in Vermont where he spent part of August 1929 with Cummings, appears in *Ms. Av, Poesía*, and in *S*, but was corrected by Humphries in *N. Ms. Av* (reprinted in *EM*, p. 202) contains autobiographical references omitted in the later versions; e.g., lines 37–48: "I want to cry speaking my name, / Federico García Lorca, on the shore of this lake, / to speak truly as a man of blood / killing in myself the mockery and the suggestive power of the word. // Here, before the extremely naked water, / I search for my freedom, my human love, / not my future flight, light or quicklime, / my present time, watching for me on the ball of crazed air. // Pure poetry. Impure poetry. / Vain pirouette, torn newspaper. / Tower of saltpeter, where words collide / and a smooth dawn which stays afloat with the anguish of exactitude." The epigraph is line 1146 of the Second Eclogue of Garcilaso de la Vega. Variants: line 3 La adivino *N, H*; la que vino *Ms. Av, S*. Line 4 bajo los frágiles helechos *N, H*; sobre los frágiles helechos *Ms. Av, S*. If *S* were correct, the lines would read: ". . . which *came*, lapping at my feet / *upon/over* the moist and fragile ferns."

Cielo vivo / Living Sky. Published posthumously in Adolfo Salazar, "El mito de Caimito," *Carteles* (Havana), Jan. 23, 1938, p. 24, following a manuscript which Lorca left in Cuba in 1930. In the upper right-hand corner of the *Ms.*, Lorca has given his own opinion of the poem: "Bueno." The *Ms.* is dated "cabaña de Dew-Kum-Inn. Edem Mills—Vermont— 24 de agosto—1929," a reference to the lakeside cottage rented by the Cummings family. See Ian Gibson, *Federico García Lorca 2. De Nueva York a Fuente Grande* (1929–36) (Barcelona: Grijalbo, 1987), p. 40. Cummings told Kessel Schwartz that the poem (or perhaps only the title) "was inspired by a night of brilliant aurora borealis activity as the lake reflected the lights against a pitch-black Mount Norris" (K. Schwartz, "García Lorca and Vermont," *Hispania* XLII [1959], p. 52). Variants: the order of *Ms.* stanzas 3 and 4 is reversed in *N, S,* and *H.* It is not possible to tell whether this is an error or a change authorized by Lorca.

El niño Stanton / Little Stanton. Unpublished during Lorca's lifetime. There are two manuscripts of the poem in the archives: a handwritten first draft, dated January 5, 1930, and a typewritten copy, destined for publication, but filled with autograph corrections. On the back of the typewritten *Ms.* is the *Tierra y luna* list. Another early version was published by Adolfo Salazar in *Carteles* (Havana), Jan. 23, 1938, p. 30.

Vaca / Cow. Published in *Revista de Occidente* (Madrid) XXXI, no. 91 (Jan. 1931), pp. 24–25, with a dedication to Lorca's friend the architect Luis Lacasa (the dedication was omitted by Bergamín in *S*).

Niña ahogada en el pozo / Little Girl Drowned in the Well. First published in Gerardo Diego, *Poesía española,* 1932. A version entitled "Niña ahogada en un pozo," and unknown to previous editors, appeared in *Ercilla* V, no. 138 (1937), p. 17 (*E*). It follows a manuscript given by Lorca to a Chilean woman identified by the editor as "M.E. de E." The *Ms.* in the Lorca archives, dated December 8, 1929, bears the title "Estatua" ("Statue"), which Lorca crossed out when substituting the final title. Variants: line 23 de su casta ignorancia *Ms., E;* de tu propia ignorancia, *N, H. GP* attributes the *N* reading to an error in the manuscript Bergamín received from F.G.L. The *Ms.* reading is restored here: "its [the well's] chaste ignorance" makes more sense than imagining the girl as a "nymph [or sprite] of her own ignorance."

Muerte / Death. First published in *Revista de Occidente* XXXI, no. 91 (Jan. 1931), pp. 21–22, with a dedication to the journalist and critic Luis de la Serna. The later dedication to Isidoro de Blas was omitted by Bergamín.

Nocturno del hueco / Nocturne of Emptied Space. First published in *Caballo verde para la poesía* (Madrid) 1 (Oct. 1935), pp. 6–8 (*CV*). The text has been a matter of much dispute. See Daniel Eisenberg, *"PNY": historia y problemas,* pp. 150–52, and *GP,* p. 734. Hernández follows *CV,* explaining that Humphries's text "appears to be a defective and unrevised copy of a manuscript, perhaps an earlier stage of the *Caballo verde* version" (*H*, 135). The poem is published in *CV* with the note: "From the unpublished book *Poet in New York.*"

Paisaje con dos tumbas y un perro asirio / Landscape with Two Graves and an Assyrian Dog. First published in *1616* VII (1935), pp. 4–5, a poetry magazine edited in London by Manuel Altolaguirre.

Ruina / Ruin. Published in *Revista de Occidente* XXXI, no. 91 (Jan. 1931), p. 22, and in Gerardo Diego, *Poesía española*, 1932, pp. 318–20. The *Revista* version is dedicated to the guitarist Regino Sainz de la Maza, a dedication omitted by Bergamín. *H* restores three lines (16–18) omitted in *N*; he suspects this stanza may have been bracketed by Lorca for *possible* omission; the poet would have decided later whether to include it or not. See F.G.L., *Antología poética*, ed. Mario Hernández, pp. 146–47.

Luna y panorama de los insectos / Moon and Panorama of the Insects. The *Ms.* is dated January 4, 1930. Lorca's epigraph is from the "Canción del pirata" ("Pirate's Song") of the Romantic poet José de Espronceda, a poem every Spanish schoolchild knows by heart. The poem's original titles were "Aventuras idiotas del capitán John" ("Idiotic Adventures of Captain John") and "Noche de luna y panorama de los insectos" ("Moonlit Night and Panorama of the Insects"). The *Ms.* contains several mentions, later omitted, of "Captain John," who is presumably a pirate (a reference to Long John Silver of *Treasure Island*?), but also a football player (one of the rejected lines reads: "Jhon [*sic*] del ruby," *ruby* being Lorca's spelling of "rugby").

Nueva York (Oficina y denuncia) / New York (Office and Denunciation). First published in *Revista de Occidente* XXXI, no. 91 (Jan. 1931), pp. 25–28, with a dedication to Fernando Vela, a frequent contributor to that journal.

Cementerio judío / Jewish Cemetery. Unpublished during Lorca's lifetime. The *Ms.*, entitled "Sepulcro judío," is dated January 18, 1930.

Crucifixión / Crucifixion. When Lorca was preparing the manuscript of *PNY*, he found he had given away his only copy of the manuscript of this poem. It was published for the first time by Miguel Benítez Inglott in *Planas de poesía* (Las Palmas, Canary Islands) IX, 1950, pp. 20–23. *H* transcribes directly from a photocopy of the manuscript.

Grito hacia Roma / Cry to Rome. Unpublished during Lorca's lifetime.

The *Ms.*, entitled "Roma," is undated. The poem is widely believed to have been inspired by the signing of the Lateran treaties between Mussolini and Pius XI in February 1929. John K. Walsh believes that "the poem is not about the Italian concordat, an event of months earlier, for which we have no record of Lorca's passion, but about the pope's failure to act humanely in the matter of the Cristeros rebellion in Mexico: on June 21, 1929, he issued the bland requisites of capitulation, leaving the Cristeros stranded in their cause, and their leader (Father Pedroza) to be killed brutally by the federalist army. I suspect that Lorca wrote the poem (probably in the summer of 1929) after having his head pumped full of indignation by friends in New York [Gabriel García Maroto, Emilio Amero, María Antoineta Rivas] who were close to the politics of Mexico" ("The Social and Sexual Geography," p. 4). Variants: line 54 melones de dinamita *N*; melenas de dinamita *S*. Depending on one's reading of the manuscript, which is not very clear, the image is either "melons of dynamite" or "long hair of dynamite."

Oda a Walt Whitman / Ode to Walt Whitman. Published in an edition of fifty copies by Ediciones Alcancía, Mexico, August 15, 1933. A fragment was reprinted in Gerardo Diego, *Poesía española. Antología (Contemporáneos)* (Madrid: Signo, 1934), pp. 441–43. The manuscript, reproduced in facsimile by Martínez Nadal in *Autógrafos, I*, pp. 205–17, is dated June 15 [1930], and must, therefore, have been finished on board the ship which took Lorca from Havana back to New York and thence to Cádiz.

Pequeño vals vienés / Little Viennese Waltz. First published in *1616* I (1934). Another version (version *T* in *EM*) is dated February 13, 1930. This poem and the next were to have formed part of a book which Lorca was planning in 1933: *Porque te quiero a ti solamente (Tanda de valses): Because I Love Only You (Set of Waltzes)*. In October 1933 he told the Argentine critic Pablo Suero: "In this book I speak of many things I like but which people say are out of fashion. Fashion I detest. Why shouldn't I admit that I like Zorrilla, that I like Chopin, that I like waltzes? . . . The book is written in waltz time . . . like *this*, sweet, lovable, vaporous" (*OC*, Vol. III, pp. 542–43). Anderson has shown that by January 1934 the poem had been incorporated into the canon of *PNY* (then known as *Introduction to Death*) and that the idea for the waltz collection had been dropped ("Lorca's 'New York Poems,' " p. 266).

Vals en las ramas / Waltz in the Branches. Published by Manuel Altolaguirre in his magazine *Héroe* (Madrid) 1, (1932), pp. 7–8, with the dedication "To Vicente Aleixandre for his poem *The Waltz*," and in an anthology put together by Altolaguirre, *Poemas escogidos* (Havana, 1939), pp. 31–33. Aleixandre's poem is from *Espadas como labios (Swords Like Lips)*, 1932. *N* follows the *Poemas escogidos* version in omitting lines 29–32. *H* follows a previously unknown version dated August 21, 1931, in the Huerta de San Vicente.

Son de negros en Cuba / Blacks Dancing to Cuban Rhythms. Written in Havana, this *son* (an Afro-Cuban chant) was dedicated to the Cuban anthropologist Fernando Ortiz (1881–1969). First published in *Musicalia*, 11 (April–May 1930). There are two manuscript texts in the archives: the one included in the lecture on *PNY* and a separate manuscript fragment. The poem alludes to the rail trip Lorca took to Santiago de Cuba. The images in lines 12–16 refer to the cigar boxes Lorca had seen as a child: thus Romeo and Julieta, the blond hair of Fonseca, the paper sea and silver coins on the lids. Two of the labels are reproduced in Marcelle Auclair, *Enfances et mort de García Lorca* (Paris: Éditions du Seuil, 1968), p. 216.